Phenomenal Prayer

Activating who you are

Dr. Amanda H. Goodson

AMANDA GOODSON

Phenomenal Prayer
by Dr. Amanda H. Goodson

Edited by Adam Colwell's WriteWorks, LLC: Adam Colwell and Ginger Colwell
Cover Design by Jaime Anaya
Typesetting by Gretchen Dorris, Ink to Book
Published by Amanda Goodson Global

Printed in the United States of America
ISBN: 978-1-7339956-2-7
ISBN: 978-1-7339956-3-4

Table of Contents

Dedication

To my family: my husband, Lonnie, for his tireless devotion to me; my son, Jelonni, who accepts me for who I am; my mother, Mable, who kept me grounded and also loved me for who I was and brought me to life; and my sister, Yolanda, who was there for me as a confidant and a friend. My phenomenal husband, son, mother, and sister.

To Bishop Bobby R. Best and Apostle Laura Thompson for their extraordinary leadership and believing in me in a phenomenal way.

To Apostle Warren Anderson and his wife, Teacher Carolyn Anderson, for their faithful, tireless, and, yes, phenomenal prayers for me.

To Rosalyn Chapple, thank you for your phenomenal work in helping me bring these teachings together for this book.

To my phenomenal Lord, who empowered me to teach the truth of His Word about prayer in this book to the best of my ability. I'm still learning and growing in my knowledge and delivery of His love and truth, and I praise Him for His faithfulness.

1

Fundamentals of Prayer

"One day Jesus was praying in a certain place. When he finished, one of his disciples said to him, 'Lord, teach us to pray, just as John taught his disciples.'"

Luke 11:1

P rayer can be many things to many people—and has been from ancient times to the modern day. But when someone asks, "What is prayer?" the answer has always been the same.

PRAYER DEFINED

Prayer is to have a spiritual communication with the Lord. It is a conversation with God. As with any human conversation, when you converse with the Lord, you can anticipate that He will respond to you. This conversation with

God can happen anywhere, at any time, and in any of life's everyday moments.

There was one afternoon when I asked my husband Lonnie to take out the trash and tend to some other things that he normally took care of around the house. Usually, he jumps right on such things, but on this day, he didn't. I kept asking, and the more I did, the angrier I got, but Lonnie is so smooth and cool, there are times nothing seems to move him. It is endearing but can sometimes be frustrating.

So, I decided I was going to get back at Lonnie and not do something I knew he wanted me to do. *That'll teach him*, I thought petulantly.

Then I heard the Lord converse with me. He said, "Why are you mad at me?"

I stopped dead in my tracks. "God, I'm not mad at you," I silently replied. "I'm mad at Lonnie because he won't do what I want him to do when I want him to do it." Then, to clarify, I repeated reverently, "I'm not mad at you, Lord. I'm mad at Lonnie."

God responded, "When you are mad at Lonnie, you are mad at me. I made him. He is my son. I am molding and shaping him to be what I want him to be. Sometimes he might not move on your timetable because I am teaching him *my* timetable. I need you to honor him, and I don't want you mad at me. He is your brother, and I need you to treat him like he is your brother, so stop being angry."

I had only one response to His loving rebuke.

"Yes, sir." I repented and didn't go back.

Another time I conversed with God and He responded in a significant way was when I was at the hairdresser. There was another lady there to get her hair done—and I received an unction from the Lord to speak to her. Sometimes God speaks to me about things going on in the lives of other people, and this was one of those moments.

Even though I had never met the woman before, I introduced myself and, just as God had instructed, boldly asked, "Do you have any sisters?"

"No," she answered matter-of-factly. It was evident she'd been asked the question before. "I only have brothers, and I'm the oldest."

"You get to tell them what to do, huh?"

She smiled. "Yep."

I excused myself and went into the bathroom. "God, you told me to ask about her sister, but she doesn't have any. Why did you tell me to do that?"

He didn't respond.

"God, can you hear me? She said she doesn't have any sisters. Why are you asking me to ask her about her sisters if she doesn't have any?"

He still said nothing, but I just knew God wasn't wrong, and was convinced I had correctly heard him moments earlier. I returned to the salon and went back up to the woman.

"Do you have anyone that you call a 'sister?'" I asked.

"Yeah," she said, "I've got a few friends that are like sisters."

"Well, God told me to ask you that question, but I told Him that you said you don't have sisters, only brothers."

She leaned back in her chair. "God said it, huh? Well, let me hear what else God has to say."

Wow, I thought to myself, then silently told God, "She's asking. She's asking. What do you want me to say?"

He said, "Ask her about Johnson."

"Do you know anybody named 'Johnson?'"

Her eyes got as big as saucers. "That's my good friend. She is in trouble. I'm supposed to be calling her, and I haven't called yet."

I said, "God says you need to call her."

She almost fell out of her seat.

Whether it's about something happening to you or in the life of someone else, when you converse with God, it is an important and intimate conversation. In fact, I believe prayer is the *intercourse of the soul* with God—not in contemplation or meditation, but in direct address to Him. This can be expressed through thoughts, spoken or written words, and even song. It can be occasional or constant, and it can be spontaneous or formal. However it happens, prayer assumes your belief in the lovingkindness, grace, steadfastness, and excellent mercy of God, in His ability and willingness to have intimate conversation with us, and in His personal control of all things, all His creatures, and all of their actions.

> **Prayer is the *intercourse* of the soul with God.**

My most intimate communications with the Lord often occur when I am preparing my sermons. Because I want to represent Him fully when I am preaching, I want to be one with Him—to intercourse with my Lord—so I can be one with His thoughts and His ways. In February 2019, as pastor of Trinity Temple CME Church in Tucson, Arizona, I was underway in a sermon series called "I Was Born to Dream," focusing on God's purpose and call on your life. Each week, I taught about a specific person from the Bible and how God had called them, and my message that week was about the

Old Testament character of Jonah. As I studied the biblical text, I learned that Nineveh, the city where God called Jonah to go and preach, was about 800 miles due east of where Jonah was located when he received God's directive.

The Lord then spoke to me. "Amanda, look up what city is 800 miles east of Tucson."

I was one with the Lord and desired to be sensitive to His thoughts and ways, no matter how unusual they may seem. I did what He asked, and discovered that the city was Abilene, Texas.

That Sunday at the close of the message, I gave everyone in the congregation something to do during the next week, a task born out of my intimate communication with God.

"Abilene, Texas is going to be our prayer assignment," I declared. "I looked up their government and their town. They've got a daddy-daughter dance coming up, so we can pray for the daddies and the daughters that they would have good relationships and that the daughters would turn out to be faithful citizens of the Kingdom. Go look it up yourself and find something about Abilene that you want to pray about. I've already given you one thing. We want to pray for their government. We want to pray for their homeless. We want to pray for the people that are in prison. We want to pray for marriages. You pick it, but Abilene, Texas is the place we are going to pray for."

One of the women in church that week, Kim, had been looking a long time for employment as a human resources director. She had gone on several interviews but had yet to get a position. The day after the service, Kim texted me and revealed that someone had sent her an email about a human resource opening—for the city government of Abilene,

Texas. "I had just finished praying for Abilene," she typed. "Do you think God wants me to move there?"

"No," I responded. "This is your seed. God is giving you an opportunity to participate in His relationship with you." I then directed her to pray for those who had already applied for that job. "Everything you want God to do for you, pray for God to do it for them. That is going to be the seed to plant the tree in the orchard for you. As you plant a seed, you get a harvest."

Kim did exactly what I said and then some. She prayed through every part of the job description she had received, for the municipality of Abilene from the police and fire departments to the mayor, and for the individuals who were in the running for the position—and guess what happened? The following week, she was offered the *exact* same job for the City of Tucson government. She planted a seed of prayer for Abilene, and God harvested that seed for her in Tucson.

In addition to being communication with God and an intercourse for the soul, prayer is a way to *honor and glorify* the Lord as you spend time with Him. God wants to be respected, revered, and honored. When I pray, I tell the Lord, "I respect you. I honor you. I adore you. I am in awe of you. When I wake up in the morning, you are the first person I think about. You put a smile on my face. You put a pep in my step. I am so glad that you thought enough about me to allow me to be your daughter. You are such a good Father. I'm in awe of you because you think so much of me."

I spread it on thick—and I believe it. I tell Him about Himself. "Look at how big you are. Your love is high. It's wide. It's deep. It has depth. God, you are amazing. You are higher than the highest mountain, and you are deeper than the deepest sea. You are such a loyal and faithful God. You are such a righteous God. You think about me every day, and I honor you for that. No one is greater that you, and no one should get thanks over you. I don't have enough words to express how much I adore you, but I'm gonna give you the words that I have." When I pray like this to honor the Lord, I find that I can treat my husband better. I can treat my son better. I can treat everybody better when I honor God first.

God also wants glory. To glorify is to lift one up and showing the weightiness of the one to whom you are bringing glory. It is like taking a budding flower and putting water on it. It blooms into its full form. In prayer, I speak to the Lord of His weightiness, of the strong hand of God and of mighty arm of God being vigilant and ready. I speak of the illumination of God and of the majesty of who He is. If you look at the sky, it speaks of God's limitless majesty and unending presence. It never ends, for He is eternal. That is glory!

As we define prayer, it is vital to recognize that prayer is not principally designed for you to selfishly ask God for things, but it is a two-way relationship in which you should talk to God and listen to Him. Think of a child's conversation with his father or mother. It is natural for a child to ask his parents for the things he needs, but parents also desire their children to listen to what they have to say.

When my son was a young teen, he loved cars and talked about his dream car's make and model. As he approached driving age, he wanted to get the car he wanted. His father told him, "Son, I want you to have that, but you are not old enough or ready to handle it yet." My husband, Lonnie, reminded our son that at a certain age he'd get a driver's permit, then a license, and then a safe car—safer than the fast sports car he wanted to drive. My son loved drifting, the technique where the driver intentionally oversteered, losing traction in the rear wheels or all four tires while maintaining control and driving the car through a corner. Lonnie and I didn't love the idea of him drifting. We were going to make sure his need for a car was met, but we were also going to keep him safe.

In the same way, there are times that we ask for things in prayer, but God knows it's too soon for us to have it, or that it may not be suitable for our purpose in Him. The Lord knows our purpose because He mapped it into us from the beginning of time. He knew us in our mother's womb (Psalm 139:13), knows who He created us to be, and won't do anything to harm us. God wants us to have tremendous things, exceedingly abundantly above all that we can ask or think (Ephesians 3:20). But He does not want us to have something outside of our destiny or beyond our capacity to handle it.

That's why we need to listen and obey His direction. Prayer is not one-directional, with you doing all the talking to God. It is bi-directional, with you listening to what God has to tell you. The Lord will speak to you in many ways: through His written Word in the Bible, through other people, through circumstances, through any aspect of His creation such as nature and animals (Psalm 19:1, Numbers 22:28), and most especially through His Holy Spirit, who has the ability to put specific words and thoughts into your mind and can even communicate to you via audible words. (See 1 Samuel 3:4-14, Psalm 18:13, Luke 3:22, Acts 9:4, and 2 Peter 1:18.)

Near the end of my time as an engineer at NASA, which was highlighted by me becoming the first African-American woman to ever hold the position of Director of Safety and Mission Assurance out of the Marshall Space Flight Center in Alabama, God spoke to me. It was 2003, not long after the Space Shuttle Columbia accident.

Here's what happened, as I wrote in my book, *Astronomical Leadership*:

I didn't hear a booming voice or see some technicolor vision. It was just an unction in my spirit that I knew was Him. He said: "I am going to ask you to do something in 2007 that is going to be the most beautiful thing you could do for me."

I wrote it down and figured it was going to be something big, where I'd be traveling, maybe worldwide. My thoughts were grandiose, but I had no more detail than that.

Meanwhile, in the wake of Columbia, an internal restructuring of the Marshall center was mandated which included my directorship position. Dr. Michael Greenfield, NASA Associate Deputy Administrator, came to Marshall to discuss where else I wanted to go within NASA. He said the organization was looking for the right place to reassign me but didn't want to put me in a role where they felt I wasn't going to be successful. He mentioned several options that he had already dismissed for that reason and said he'd get back to me.

Then, seemingly out of nowhere, I was contacted by an executive search firm hired by an engineering company in Tucson, Arizona. They were looking for someone to help with mission assurance. I took the call and told the person to call me back in a week. I used that time to gather seven referrals for colleagues I thought were ideal for the position. When the firm called back, I declined the offer and gave the person the names of the others. "I need to focus on getting the shuttle back in the air," I said, "so don't call me back. Call them."

The representative of the search firm was astonished. "This has never happened before. We've never had somebody give a job away to someone else. We're going to stay in touch with you. You are very rare and unique."

I hung up and thought nothing more about it. As far as I was concerned, I was staying at NASA. Where else could I go? I was at the highest rung I could get, other than maybe going to NASA headquarters or to Johnson in Houston or Kennedy in Florida. I was in my early forties while my peers were between 55 and 60. I had it good and I was thankful.

Then God did something utterly unexpected. He began to tug on my heart that He wanted me to actually go to Tucson. This was unique—the first time He directed me to move from one place to another ... To have Him lead me to relocate across the country was unusual and uncomfortable, especially considering what had just happened with Columbia. Yet God confirmed His direction and convicted me that I needed to be obedient. I also began to believe that the "most beautiful thing" He wanted me to do was contingent on me being in Tucson. When I told Lonnie about it, he agreed, and we began preparing ourselves.

In May, I contacted the executive search firm that had first called me about the job in Arizona and asked if they still had the mission assurance position available. It had been filled, though not by anyone from my referral list. They did, however, make another position available, and I told them I was interested in being interviewed for it. Shortly thereafter, they arranged for me to go to Tucson. I'd never seen the desert southwest before, and when my plane flew in over the city to land, I looked out the window and thought it was brown, grassless, dirty, and nothing like what I was used to in Alabama.

When I got to the hotel, God nudged at my heart—again.

"I need you to take another look," he said to my spirit. "I made this place. Nothing about it is ugly."

I walked over and gazed out the window—and I saw beauty emerge right before my eyes: the rolling foothills leading up to the mountains, the green-trunked desert trees, and the tall cactus. Later, when it got dark, I took in a view from those foothills at the glittering city lights. It was as though Tucson was suddenly the most beautiful place I'd ever seen.

Not only did I ended up moving to Tucson for the engineering job, but the Lord fulfilled His divine purpose for my life in another, most unanticipated way. He made me a church pastor. Again, from *Astronomical Leadership*:

> I was appointed pastor of Trinity Temple CME in June 2007, doing the "most beautiful thing" the Lord had for me in the most unlikely way I could imagine. Over a decade later, I remained pastor and had seen the congregation grow to a core group of up to 50-65 people at peak times who have learned to praise and worship God more openly, love His Word, and give to the church and back to the community. I was still at the engineering company full-time, had launched a speaking and coaching service, and had become an independent, certified John Maxwell coach, teacher, and speaker.

THE PURPOSE OF PRAYER

The first mention of people calling upon the name of the Lord in prayer is found in Genesis 4:26. That's when humanity was just starting to increase on the Earth after Cain, the oldest son of Adam and Eve, killed his younger brother Abel.

Ever since then, spanning the generations, individuals have sought the Lord, just as He has encouraged us to do in passages such as Psalm 91:15 ("He will call on me, and I will answer him; I will be with him in trouble, I will deliver him and honor him."), Isaiah 65:24 ("Before they call I will answer; while they are still speaking I will hear."), and Matthew 7:7 ("Ask and it will be given to you; seek and you will find; knock and the door will be opened to you.").

According to Scripture, some of the many purposes of prayer are to:[1]

- seek the favor of the Lord (Exodus 32:11)
- pour out your soul to God (1 Samuel 1:15)
- cry out to heaven (2 Chronicles 32:20)
- seek God earnestly and plead with Him (Job 8:5)
- draw near to the Lord (Psalms 73:28)
- kneel before the Father in humility (Ephesians 3:14)

Yet some people ask, "If God is omniscient and already knows our wants and needs, why is prayer necessary?" In addition to the many benefits brought out earlier as prayer was defined, prayer is vital because it requires us to *exercise our faith*, trusting that God hears us and answers us according to His good will and love for us.

My father had a heart condition, and he eventually contracted a virus that led to the congestive heart failure which took his life. Because of that, I decided to have my heart checked and was diagnosed with mitral valve prolapse in 2000. When I saw a cardiologist, I was told that while my leaky heart valve wasn't severe enough to require medication, it was serious enough to regularly monitor.

I started getting an annual echocardiogram. I also began praying for healing. In an additional exercise of my faith, I told my doctor that God was going to heal me.

"I just want to go on the record," I said.

"Yeah, yeah," he responded nonchalantly. "Come back in six months or a year."

I did exactly that for several years, in Alabama and then after I had moved to Arizona. Each time I went in, the echocardiogram was done and showed mild to medium valve leakage—and with each visit, I repeated my declaration of healing to my doctor.

Then, about seven years after my original diagnosis, I had

the test done again. After it was completed, the doctor came in. He then thumbed through some papers, and as he did, he started shaking his head. He looked like he was in shock. "I thought you had a problem with your heart," he said. Obviously, he knew I did, but the way he worded his statement showed how surprised he was. He kept looking at one paper, then the next, then back at me, then at the papers again. It was like he couldn't believe what he was reading.

"But I've got news for you. You don't have a leaky valve any more, and you don't have to come back, unless you feel uncomfortable and want to come back."

I sat on the exam table, swinging my legs back and forth like a little girl. I knew what had happened. God had heard and answered my prayer. I was healed!

"Nah, I won't come back," I responded, "at least not for that, anyway."

Still dumbfounded, the doctor excused himself. After he departed and closed the door, I hopped down from the table and started raising the roof for Jesus! I tried not to be too loud because I didn't necessarily want to disturb the other patients, but I raised my hands and danced all over that room, praising God. It was amazing!

Through that experience—and by staying faithful in prayer for all those years, never wavering in my belief in Him—I discovered that I could speak to a mountain called mitral valve prolapse, and it would obey my faith! It's not that I didn't believe in healing before. I did. But this was personal because it was a generational condition that was broken by the power of God in response to my prayers. In this case, the purpose of my prayers was to break the curse of heart disease in my family.

WHY WE ARE TO PRAY

I've identified five main reasons in Scripture why we are to pray. Each one is uniquely compelling and life-changing.

1. **We are commanded to pray.** As disciples of Christ, we ought to be praying people. Because Christ is our mediator to the Father, we are to conform ourselves to His image and conduct, doing what is acceptable in His sight. Paul tells us more in 1 Timothy 2:1-7:

"I urge, then, first of all, that petitions, prayers, intercession and thanksgiving be made for all people—for kings and all those in authority, that we may live peaceful and quiet lives in all godliness and holiness. This is good, and pleases God our Savior, who wants all people to be saved and to come to a knowledge of the truth. For there is one God and one mediator between God and mankind, the man Christ Jesus, who gave himself as a ransom for all people. This has now been witnessed to at the proper time. And for this purpose I was appointed a herald and an apostle—I am telling the truth, I am not lying—and a true and faithful teacher of the Gentiles."

Prayer is vital because it requires us to exercise *our faith.*

We find more commands from the Bible to pray for our enemies and those who persecute us (Matthew 5:44), to be ready to pray at any time (Mark 13:33), to not give up in prayer (Luke 18:1), to pray in the Spirit on all occasions with all kinds of requests for all the Lord's people (Ephesians 6:18), to be faithful in prayer (Romans 12:12), to devote ourselves to prayer while being watchful and thankful (Colossians 4:2), and to pray continually (1 Thessalonians 5:17).

How hard or easy it is to obey God's command to pray depends on the circumstances. It's easy for some people because they know what God can do. It's hard when someone is not disciplined, and they don't have faith because they don't understand the communication channel that prayer offers us. Faith is the "Kingdom currency" that our prayer rides on to make the answer come.

Some have a conflict between their heart and their head. The head is where we think and act in power. Our heart is where we have our character. Sometimes our heart wants to pray but our head doesn't. Other times our head knows we ought to pray and our heart is not in it. The key is to get the two of them connected. Once we see that intersection between the heart and the head, between belief and discipline, we can really soar. It gets better, too, with maturity. Prayer becomes part of the fiber of your very being, and you gain the wisdom to know you can't leave home without prayer.

2. We are *invited* to pray. Prayer is an invitation to participate in conversation and communion with the Lord. It is not to be thought of as a task or duty that we are obligated to carry out, but as a loving summons from the Lord to interact with Him, which is motivated by the realization that we love God because He first loved us (1 John 4:10). Therefore, the invitation to pray is an invitation to love. Our prayers are not our gift to God, but rather His gift to us so that we can be delivered in the day of trouble (Psalm 50:15), listened to by Him (Jeremiah 29:12), and exercise our faith by asking, seeking, knocking, and receiving the good gifts He has for us (Matthew 7:7-11).

When I'm in the workplace, my supervisors often invite me to participate in meetings with them. He or she has an agenda and expects me to show up, especially if I am *on* that agenda to provide information, or if there is information they are going to be sharing, that I need to know. I am invited and expected to attend and be involved. Likewise, God, your boss, has an agenda for you. He wants you to hear Him. He wants you to talk to Him and tell Him your agenda. It is open, two-way communication between you and the Creator of the universe that you can access 24-7—and it is glorious.

3. We are to *respond* to prayer. Not only are we are summoned to pray, but we are to respond because God loves us and desires relationship with us. When He calls us to something, then we are to answer the same way the prophet Isaiah did by saying, "Here am I." (Isaiah 6:8) When we respond to God in prayer, it is not only an act of obedience, but it is also our way of giving honor to the One who gave His all for us.

One of the reasons we sometimes don't respond is because we think God is going to ask us to do something that is too hard to accomplish. Yet before He asks us to do anything, He has already weighed it out. In 1 Corinthians 2:10, we are told that the Holy Spirit "searches all things, even the deep things of God." Prior to calling you to you "what no eye has seen" or "what no ear has heard" (1 Corinthians 1:9), God has already searched it out and determined that you can do it. Before it is dropped into the earthly realm, He has already decided it to be so. Yet we so easily distort what He is calling us to do and magnify it into a bigger issue than it really is. We imagine something that is not there instead of seeing, by faith, what is really there.

It is kind of like when I plug in my earphones to listen to the radio. The radio is always playing. The frequency is always there. But it's not until I plug in my earphones that I can hear—and then I can decide whether or not I like what the station is playing or if it is exactly what I needed to hear.

When God calls to you in prayer, respond in faith. Hear what He wants you to hear. See what He wants you to see. Be confident that He has already done everything necessary for you to achieve what He is asking you to do.

4. **We are to *experience power* in prayer.** The power in prayer does not come from the act of praying, but from the One to whom we pray. Within the confines of our humanity, we are blessed to be able to reach beyond and upward to God, knowing that He hears us and will act.

Christ put it this way in John 14:13-14:

"And I will do whatever you ask in my name, so that the Father may be glorified in the Son. You may ask me for anything in my name, and I will do it."

In His divine omnipotence, He responds in power and we receive His strength. This power from God unleashes us to live our lives in service to Him as well as to others, and we can rely on the fact that He will give us everything we need. As 1 John 5:14-15 declares:

"This is the confidence we have in approaching God: that if we ask anything according to his will, he hears us. And if we know that he hears us—whatever we ask—we know that we have what we asked of him."

James 5:15 promises us that our faith-driven prayers can manifest His power to do the miraculous. In November 2018, I was invited to a revival at a church in Los Angeles, California. God placed on my heart the need to pray for people with vertigo. One woman came up to the altar, but another lady, whose vertigo had left her deaf in one ear for 10 years, remained seated. The next night, though, she approached me. "I should've responded last night. If you can, I'd like you to pray for me." She told me about the deafness and the virus, and then we laid hands on her and prayed. Other intercessors joined me. I repeatedly whispered in her ear, "Can you hear me now? If you can hear me, say a word or raise your hand." She didn't reply, so we kept praying.

Then, all of a sudden, she said of her ear, "It feels like it is plugged up." We kept seeking God. Her pastor was talking to her right behind her. After a few more moments, he declared, "Thank you, Jesus!" She said, "Oh my God, I can hear!" Her hearing was restored, and it's been that way ever since.

That's not the only time I've seen God's power flow through prayer. At a service in Phoenix, Arizona, a woman who'd had a series of strokes and couldn't get anywhere without a walker was healed. She ended up dancing all over the place! Another time, during a prayer call on the phone, a woman revealed that her son was in the ICU in a diabetic coma. His blood sugar reading was over 1,300 milligrams per deciliter. (A normal reading is less than 140 mg/dL) The doctors said his brain should have already shut down. We prayed for him—and he came out of the coma! His blood sugar plummeted to around 100 mg/dL. He was later removed from all of his medications. The diabetes vanished.

As the old hymn, written and composed by Lewis Edgar

Jones, attests, "There is power, power, wonder-working power / In the precious blood of the Lamb."

5.   **We are to *follow* Christ's example to pray.** Since we are created in the image and likeness of God (Genesis 1:27), we are to "be conformed to the image of his Son." (Romans 8:29) Jesus prayed because He was living in a human body and, therefore, had to set aside His divinity (Philippians 2:7). Just like it is for us, prayer was the way Jesus the Son communicated with God the Father, and He did it often (Matthew 14:23 and 26:36, Mark 1:35, Luke 5:16 and 6:12).

The main reason, though, that Jesus prayed was for connection. He and the Father were one spiritually. Christ was compassionate because He loved His Father. He was commissioned because He was committed to get instruction and to keep in touch with His Father. Jesus understood eternity and knew He needed constant direction from the eternal God. If Christ needed all of this, how much more do we need it from God?

THE ORDER OF PRAYER

When we pray, there are five expressions that, when presented in order to the Lord, will infuse our prayers with power and purpose: adoration, confession, thanksgiving, supplication, and intercession.

When we start our prayers with **adoration**, think of it like arriving home each day after work. We don't just rush in, head straight for the refrigerator, and make ourselves a sandwich. We say hello to our spouse or other family members. We acknowledge them and let them know they are important. In the same way, we greet and address our

Lord when we begin prayer with adoration. We let Him know there is nothing more important than acknowledging Him first. Jesus modeled this for us in His teaching about prayer during His Sermon of the Mount. In Matthew 6:9, He said, "This, then, is how you should pray: 'Our Father in heaven, hallowed be your name." The word "hallowed" means "greatly revered and honored." Isn't that great? Christ didn't ask for anything else in that prayer until *after* He addressed His Father as being holy.

Through adoration, we give God the honor and respect that is His due, worshiping Him for who He is, not for what He can do for us. Adoration *ascribes* to God what He made, what He owns, and that He is the source. It involves telling God how much we love and appreciate Him, which powerfully centers our focus on God, allowing us to see Him as mighty and awesome (Psalm 68:35).

Adoration may not come easily for those who are not accustomed to doing it. It's hard to learn how to ascribe to God if you spend most of your day complaining. You may need time to develop new habits that position you to offer adoration to the Lord. But once you begin, and then do it the next day and the next, you'll find that adoration will become a natural part of who you are.

Here are some practical steps to learn how to adore God:[2]

- Determine in your heart that you will do this daily in all the circumstances of your life. Ask Him for His grace and power to help you live out this commitment.
- Saturate yourself with God's Word. It will fuel a lifestyle of adoration. Your knowledge of God will determine the depth of your adoration of Him.
- Develop a vocabulary of adoration. Sometimes you

21

don't adore God because you do not know the words to say. Yet when you learn about God and grow in your understanding of Him by studying His characteristics, His names, and His titles, you create a vocabulary from which to adore the Lord. "God, you are a loving God. You are kind. You are faithful." When you look at His names, you can declare, "You are Jehovah-Rapha, the God who heals," or "You are Jehovah-Nissi, my banner." With His titles, you can speak, "I adore you because you are Master and Lord."

- Turn every truth about God into a statement. I adore Him because He won't lie. He is a righteous judge. He is merciful and good. These are truths that you can personalize for your situation.
- Start an adoration journal. Record what you learn about God, write them down daily, and meditate upon them.
- Say, "I love you" to the Lord as often as you can. He loves you and desires to hear you tell Him that you love Him.

I start each day with adoration to God. The Lord wants to be wooed and hear nice things about Himself. When I wake up in the morning, He is first on my mind and in my heart. I'll say, "God, I am so in awe of your Word that I want to read it so I can know you better, clearer, and stronger. I love when people talk about you, Lord. I am in awe of the fact that when people mention your name, I want to hear more about you."

The late, great Kingdom leader Myles Munroe was a strong influence on my life. He helped me learn so much about Kingdom leadership: what it means and what God has purposed us to do in it. He taught that it all begins with adoring God and putting Him in His proper place in my heart and mind. He helped me discover that when I adore God, He gives me new revelation about what I ascribe to Him because adoration opens me up to know the Lord in a deeper way.

Confession is the next step of prayer where we specifically tell God where we have fallen short, and then ask for His guidance and strength to turn away from any future temptations. Confession involves proclaiming the truth of God's Word in the face of opposition and trouble. It is in confession where we are fully honest before God by not cherishing or hiding sin in our hearts (Psalm 66:18; Isaiah 59:1-2) and by allowing Him to search and test us (Psalm 139:23-24).

The process of discovering the sin that is breaking our communion with the Lord can be quite painful. However, once it is discovered, confession sets it right with God. It is where we purposely seek the Holy Spirit's conviction for our sin so we can ask God for forgiveness and then trust Him to cleanse us by the blood

> **Just like it is for us, prayer was the way Jesus the Son communicated with God the Father.**

of His Son, Jesus. Our willingness to seek forgiveness for our sins ensures that our prayers will not be hindered by those sins (1 John 1:9).

Christ's parable of the prodigal son (Luke 15:11-32) provides a beautiful picture of someone brought to confession. The youngest son of a wealthy father received his share of the estate early, and then went off and squandered his inheritance on lascivious living. The Bible picks up his story:

"After he had spent everything, there was a severe famine in that whole country, and he began to be in need. So he went and hired himself out to a citizen of that country, who sent him to his fields to feed pigs. He longed to fill his stomach with the pods that the pigs were eating, but no one gave him anything. When he came to his senses, he said, 'How many of my father's hired servants have food to spare, and here I am starving to death! I will set out and go back to my father and say to him: Father, I have sinned against heaven and against you. I am no longer worthy to be called your son; make me like one of your hired servants.'" Luke 15:14-19

Instead of "came to his senses," other translations say the son "came to himself." I like that. He was brought to a place where he recognized the image and the likeness that God had placed in him. He also understood who his father was, and that he was willing to go and serve him. So, he went back home and confessed his sin to his father—but instead of condemning his son or making him a servant, the joy-filled dad celebrated his son's return and restored him to relationship with him.

That's exactly what the Lord does for us when we confess our sins. He welcomes us, loves us, and brings us back into fellowship with Him.

Thanksgiving, the third step in the order of prayer, is the acknowledgement that all blessings come from God alone. It involves thanking Him for past blessings we have received as well as for future blessings that we anticipate. Thanksgiving shows our gratitude, brings glory to Him (Psalm 69:30), and gives us incredible peace of mind. Philippians 4:6-7 declares:

> *"Do not be anxious about anything, but in every situation, by prayer and petition, with thanksgiving, present your requests to God. And the peace of God, which transcends all understanding, will guard your hearts and your minds in Christ Jesus."*

Psalms 100:4 exhorts us to "enter his gates with thanksgiving and his courts with praise; give thanks to him and praise his name." There are a number of ways we can give thanksgiving to God by:

- Remembering Him. This happens in our daily thoughts, words, and deeds.
- Recognizing Him and specifically counting our blessings.
- Repenting of our sins daily. This shows God our gratitude, cleanses us, and makes us worthy to receive additional blessings.
- Obeying His commandments.
- Choosing to be humble. Pride leads to ingratitude, but humility leads to gratefulness (Luke 18:9-14).

One time when I was preaching on the East coast, I asked everyone to write down on an index card three things they wanted God to do for them over the weekend. Next, I told every person there we were going to thank Him for taking care of those needs ahead of time. We placed them in an envelope and laid it on the altar before God. Before the weekend was over, one lady ended up with a refund from the IRS that she'd been waiting for a long time. That was one of the things she'd written on her card. Another lady with diabetes received resources to help her get her medicine. She had been told by the provider that it wasn't approved, and they weren't going to pay for it any longer—and that weekend she received a three-month supply of what she needed for her disease. Many others told me, "Guess what God did? Guess what was on my list?" It was wonderful to see God move on behalf of the faith-filled declarations of thanks to Him.

Supplication is where we ask God for specific things. Because we have adored, confessed, and thanked, we are now standing in the power of His presence and might. It is in supplication where the mighty armor of God triumphs. We successfully wrestle against Satan and his forces, bind the works of darkness that are in opposition to God's purposes, and watch and persevere with full faith and awareness of God's work in Christ for us—knowing that His Spirit will lead us to total victory. Ephesians 6:10-18 exhorts:

"Finally, be strong in the Lord and in his mighty power. Put on the full armor of God, so that you can take your stand against the devil's schemes. For our struggle is not against flesh and blood, but against the rulers, against the authorities, against the powers of this dark world and against the spiritual forces of evil in the heavenly realms. Therefore put on the full armor of God, so that when the day of evil comes, you may be able to stand your ground, and after you have done everything, to stand. Stand firm then, with the belt of truth buckled around your waist, with the breastplate of righteousness in place, and with your feet fitted with the readiness that comes from the gospel of peace. In addition to all this, take up the shield of faith, with which you can extinguish all the flaming

arrows of the evil one. Take the helmet of salvation and the sword of the Spirit, which is the word of God. And pray in the Spirit on all occasions with all kinds of prayers and requests. With this in mind, be alert and always keep on praying for all the Lord's people."

One of the greatest stories of supplication in all of Scripture is found in 1 Samuel 1. Hannah was a woman in great anguish. She was unable to have a child and wanted to have a son more than anything. She also practiced supplication, crying out to God for years, often without eating, waiting for Him to act according to His purposes for her. She knew He was a God who could do the impossible.

So, despite scorn and discouragement, Hannah emptied her heart to the Lord, promising to dedicate her son to God's service. One day, as Eli the priest observed the depth of her faithful supplication, he told Hannah, "Go in peace, and may the God of Israel grant you what you have asked of him." She then "went her way and ate something, and her face was no longer downcast." (1 Samuel 1:17-18) Not long after, Hannah bore a son, Samuel, and she followed through on her promise to God. She took the child to Eli and left him to be raised in the temple. She continued to have influence over the boy's life through the years, and Samuel grew up to become one of the most influential and godly prophets in the Bible. We are told that "the Lord was with Samuel as he grew up, and he let none of Samuel's words fall to the ground." (1 Samuel 3:19) When Samuel prophesied, you could count on it to come to pass because He listened to God and honored Him.

Finally, **intercession** is praying for something or someone with purposeful urgency, willing to cast all of our weaknesses before His absolute strength and power. We are to intercede with total trust and in authentic hope and expectation that God will step in and act, even if how He responds is different than we would prefer. All of us have the ability to intercede in prayer, and God eagerly wants us to intervene through intercession (Isaiah 59:16).

Imagine being in the middle of a room with three chairs lined up in a row. God is sitting on one side of the row, we are in the middle seat, and on the other side is a person or a problem. When we intercede, we turn our back on the problem or what is going on in that person's life, turn toward God, and have a conversation with Him about that individual or situation. Ezekiel 22:30 characterizes intercession as standing "in the gap," and it is something that we can do in confidence that He will answer in His mercy and grace (Hebrews 4:16).

In Genesis 18, Abraham serves as an intercessor for the people of the evil city of Sodom. The Lord told Abraham that the sin in Sodom and its neighboring town of Gomorrah was so great it was "grievous," but Abraham intervened:

"Then Abraham approached him and said: 'Will you sweep away the righteous with the wicked? What if there are fifty righteous people in the city? Will you really sweep it away and not spare the place for the sake of the fifty righteous people in it? Far be it from you to do such a thing—to kill the righteous with the wicked, treating the righteous and the wicked alike. Far be it from you! Will not the Judge of all the earth do right?' The Lord said, 'If I find fifty righteous people in the city of Sodom, I will spare the whole place for their sake.' Then Abraham spoke up again: 'Now that I have been so bold as to speak to the Lord, though I am nothing but dust and ashes, what if the number of the righteous is

five less than fifty? Will you destroy the whole city for lack of five people?' 'If I find forty-five there,' he said, 'I will not destroy it.'" (Genesis 18:23-28)

Abraham was bold—and he didn't stop there. He continued to intervene until the Lord agreed to spare Sodom for the sake of 10 righteous people. Sadly, there weren't even that many there living for God, and Sodom and Gomorrah were destroyed, though among those who fled and survived was Abraham's nephew, Lot, and his daughters.

Remember the earlier story about my congregation and prayer? We interceded for the city of Abilene, Texas. God prompted me to have us do so, and we did. The Lord may ask us to intercede for a thing, country, city, family, or person. Intercession for others is vital since each one of us has a nation attached to

All of us have the ability to intercede in prayer.

us: our spouse, children, grandchildren, and great-grandchildren. Each one of those people are going to influence other people. God allows us to see a problem—and because He is solution-focused, He asks us to step in to that situation, on behalf of that country, city, family, or person, and resolve it. Intercession is a mighty work we do on behalf of His Kingdom.

TYPES OF PRAYER

In my study and practice of prayer, I've identified and experienced six types of prayer that everyone has the ability to use. Some of us may not choose to do so because we don't know about these prayers. Often, though, it's because we don't want to pay the price. It's like not going to a certain store to buy clothes because you think it's too expensive, only to discover they have sales, too. We cannot imagine the depth, width, height, and breadth of what we can tap into through these prayers, even though God wants us to "demolish arguments and every pretension that sets itself up against the knowledge of God" and "take captive every thought to make it obedient to Christ." (2 Corinthians 10:5)

Yet we will grow our faith by operating in His Word and shutting down everything that keeps us from maturity—and these prayers allow us to know God in a greater, more intimate way. Let's look at each one.

1. **Prayer of faith.** Faith comes by hearing and hearing by the Word of God (Romans 10:17), so having His truth hidden in our hearts is essential to using the prayer of faith. The blood of Jesus is the foundation for our lives, and God's Word is the foundation for our faith. Faith is defined as the confident assurance that what we expect to happen is going to happen (Hebrews 11:1). Therefore, the prayer of faith is one that will *always* get answered. But it requires that we believe without doubt (Matthew 21:22; James 1:6), because faith cannot successfully operate where doubt is present. Jesus said in Mark 11:23-24:

> *"Truly I tell you, if anyone says to this mountain, 'Go, throw yourself into the sea,' and does not doubt in their heart but believes that what they say will happen, it will be done for them. Therefore I tell you, whatever you ask for in prayer, believe that you have received it, and it will be yours."*

The prayer of faith involves:
- Speaking and proclaiming what you want

30

- Believing what you are asking for
- Seeing yourself receiving it, and

Asking the Holy Spirit how you are then supposed to act upon your faith

One of my friends, Carolyn, is a great woman of faith and prayer. She doesn't have a lot of material or financial resources, but that doesn't stop her from believing in the One who has eternal resources. She told me of a time when she needed to get to work but didn't have any money to buy fuel for her car. She declared, "God, I am going to pray according to your Word. You know I want to go to work, and you know I need gas, and I don't have it. I am going to drive to the gas station and wait until you give it to me." She drove to the station, got out of the car, and waited by the pump until God told her, "Look under your foot." She did—and there rested a $10 bill. She got her gas and went on to work. She spoke a prayer of faith, and the money was there.

Another young woman told me about her father, a farmer and property developer, who talked to her about faith so much when she was a teenager that she got tired of it. He'd drive her around to different places and show her where he wanted to buy land. Once, she said he got out of the car and literally spoke to the land. "Dirt, you will be sold to me. You are my property. I'm gonna build on you. I'm gonna plant on you." When the land was sold to somebody else, she didn't understand. But within a short period of time, the realtor contacted her father to let him know the original buyer didn't want it—and he ended up getting the property, just like he declared he would.

2. Prayer of commitment. This prayer requires us to possess an earnest desire to live totally within the will of God. It is spoken with the unwavering knowledge that nothing is too big or small for God (Jeremiah 32:27). It also expresses a willingness to give all of our problems and situations over to the Lord, which releases you from the stress caused by your concerns.

As 1 Peter 5:7 exhorts:

"Cast all your anxiety on him because he cares for you."

When Joshua assembled all the tribes of Israel at Shechem, he summoned the elders, leaders, judges and officials to present themselves before God. Joshua then spoke to the people, declaring what the Lord had done for Abraham, Isaac, and Jacob, and recounting how God had used his predecessor Moses to lead them out of captivity in Egypt and into the Promised Land. Then Joshua said:

"Now fear the Lord and serve him with all faithfulness. Throw away the gods your ancestors worshiped beyond the Euphrates River and in Egypt, and serve the Lord. But if serving the Lord seems undesirable to you, then choose for yourselves this day whom you will serve, whether the gods your ancestors served beyond the Euphrates, or the gods of the Amorites, in whose land you are living. But as for me and my household, we will serve the Lord." (Joshua 24:14-15)

Just as Joshua boldly dedicated himself and his family to serve God and submit to His will as an example to the people of Israel, our prayers of commitment for our families and others declares our alignment to God's purposes and solidifies our trust in Him. Psalm 37:5-9 promises:

"Commit your way to the Lord; trust in him and he will do this: He will make your righteous reward shine like

the dawn, your vindication like the noonday sun. Be still before the Lord and wait patiently for him; do not fret when people succeed in their ways, when they carry out their wicked schemes. Refrain from anger and turn from wrath; do not fret—it leads only to evil. For those who are evil will be destroyed, but those who hope in the Lord will inherit the land."

When we allow it to control us, money can be one of our greatest sources of anxiety. But it becomes a vehicle of abundance and blessing when we commit to manage it according to biblical principles and leverage it to achieve God's purposes. One woman decided she was going to give the tithe, 10 percent of her income, to God through her giving to her church. She also desired to back date her giving to the beginning of the calendar year, meaning her first few donations were going to be more than 10 percent as she gave to make up the difference. At the same time, though, she didn't want to create havoc for her family or her finances because of her decision.

So, she prayed. "Lord, I commit myself, and my decision to obey your Word, to you. You have promised to take care of me and my family. I commit my resources to you, and I don't want to turn back." It wasn't easy. There were times she had to swallow hard because money was tight. But, with each week's giving, God provided. She and her family always had what they needed and learned to live just fine—better than fine, actually—off the remaining 90 percent. The Lord honored her prayer of commitment. Today, she continues to tithe and gives even more in offerings.

3.   Prayer of agreement. This occurs when two or more followers of Christ gather themselves together in prayer and are in total agreement with each other's request (Matthew 18:20).

Jesus gives us the greatest example of this, for He constantly prayed in agreement with His Father. John 17 recounts His prayer to the Father on behalf of His disciples and for all believers (you and I). He deliberately and passionately asked for God's purposes to be accomplished in and through those for whom He prayed.

Perhaps His greatest prayer of agreement, though, was in the Garden of Gethsemane. We know it well, but read it again, slowly, and appreciate it anew:

> "Then Jesus went with his disciples to a place called Gethsemane, and he said to them, 'Sit here while I go over there and pray.' He took Peter and the two sons of Zebedee along with him, and he began to be sorrowful and troubled. Then he said to them, 'My soul is overwhelmed with sorrow to the point of death. Stay here and keep watch with me.' Going a little farther, he fell with his face to the ground and prayed, 'My Father, if it is possible, may this cup be taken from me. Yet not as I will, but as you will.' Then he returned to his disciples and found them sleeping. 'Couldn't you men keep watch with me for one hour?' he asked Peter. 'Watch and pray so that you will not fall into temptation. The spirit is willing, but the flesh is weak.' He went away a second time and prayed, 'My Father, if it is not possible for this cup to be taken away unless I drink it, may your will be done.'" (Matthew 26:36-42)

That is a prayer of agreement. When we say, as individuals or as two or more people, "Nonetheless, God, I want what you want," and we stand in agreement with His Word for our life, it super exceeds whatever we could expect or imagine. It far surpasses anything we can do on our own.

I'm involved in a prayer group of men and women from all over the country, spanning four time zones, who regularly meet in the morning by phone to pray in agreement for one another. Every type of request is made during this gathering—for finances, employment, healing—and then we stop and pray. "Lord, we stand in agreement with one another that you will hear and answer our prayers and meet these needs according to your will." It's been incredible! We've seen breakthroughs and deliverances as God had responded, and continues to act, on behalf of our prayers for each other.

4. Prayer in the Spirit. This type of prayer comes from the depth of our souls and is often, but not always, accompanied by the spiritual gift of speaking in tongues (1 Corinthians 14:1-25). Our use of tongues gives us a revelation of God and an opportunity to speak to Him in a language that cannot be subverted, deciphered, or undone by Satan. Tongues are also a witness for God to others, and interpretations of tongues can be an exhortation, comfort, edification, or even prophetic.

Prayer in the Spirit goes to God the Father so that His Son Jesus may intercede for us (Romans 8:34). The Spirit then prays with us and moves us to turn to God and trust in Him for our needs, finding renewed hope. We are exhorted in Scripture to pray in the Spirit "on all occasions" (Ephesians 6:18), and when we are so burdened that we don't know what to say, prayer in the Spirit aids us. Romans 8:26 teaches:

"In the same way, the Spirit helps us in our weakness. We do not know what we ought to pray for, but the Spirit himself intercedes for us through wordless groans."

I'll never forget the time my son Jelonni got sick. He was three-and-a-half and contracted a virus that rendered him unable to retain fluids and brought on severe dehydration. As he laid there with a sullen look on his pallid face, he looked up at me, his eyes pleading, and said, "You are my Mommy. Do something."

My stomach dropped. I felt like there was nothing I could do to help him. But I did know how to pray. I don't recall everything I said, but I allowed the Spirit to pray for me as I anguished. I did not want my son to suffer or be in any more pain. As I wept, my emotions and energy were drained, but I gave everything I had to the Lord. I prayed in the Spirit, and as I did, I leaned into my mighty God. "I *am* Jelonni's Mommy, Lord, but you are my Father. Do you hear his request of me? I've done all I can do in my strength. Do something. You are my healer. I've done all I can in my power. Do something."

Within 48 hours, the virus disappeared and Jelonni fully recovered. We didn't even have to go to the hospital. I prayed in the Spirit, and the Lord heard and moved on behalf of my son.

5. Prayer of imprecation. This prayer is to be done when praying against our spiritual enemies (Ephesians 6:12), and it expresses the Lord's hatred of evil and of the wicked things done by evildoers. I do this every day, saying, "God, I rebuke the enemy that comes against my increase and the devourer that comes against anything that I am going to do today. I dispatch God's angels against the enemy, and I send them to protect me and everything that is associated with me." It is a powerful declaration!

Jesus also exhorts us to speak the prayer of imprecation for our earthly enemies, even those who seek to destroy us (Psalm 69:4), pleading for their salvation and for God's will to be done in their lives. To do so guides us toward God's highest standard for us (Matthew 5:44-48) and is an ultimate expression of His mercy through our lives. Luke 6:27-38 tells us:

> *"Love your enemies, do good to those who hate you, bless those who curse you, pray for those who mistreat you. If someone slaps you on one cheek, turn to them the other also. If someone takes your coat, do not withhold your shirt from them. Give to everyone who asks you, and if anyone takes what belongs to you, do not demand it back. Do to others as you would have them do to you. If you love those who love you, what credit is that to you? Even sinners love those who love them. And if you do good to those who are good to you, what credit is that to you? Even sinners do that. And if you lend to those from whom you expect repayment, what credit is that to you? Even sinners lend to sinners, expecting to be repaid in full. But love your enemies, do good to them, and lend to them without expecting to get anything back. Then your reward will be great, and you will be children of the Most High, because he is kind to the ungrateful and wicked. Be merciful, just as your Father is merciful."*

Prayer in the Spirit goes to God the Father so that His Son Jesus may intercede for us.

A few years ago, we remodeled the foyer area of the church, adding bathrooms and metal security doors to the entrance. Unexpected expenses on the project forced us to spend thousands on the project, beyond budget. Before the work was completed, someone broke in and stole about $2,000 worth of audio equipment. I couldn't believe it. As pastor, I was naturally surprised about what happened, and I was upset at whoever did it—but I supernaturally responded with a prayer of imprecation. "God, I ask that the thieves come to know you as Lord. I pray that whoever touches that sound board and hears those speakers would touch and hear Jesus." I believed that what they intended for evil God meant for good and that it would bring Him glory.

The prayer of imprecation for our enemies can be the most difficult prayers to speak, especially when someone has intentionally harmed you (or your children) materially, emotionally, or spiritually. Yet it is the most liberating prayer as we forgive them, bless them, and then trust God for the rest.

6. Prayer of binding and loosing. In this prayer, we exercise the spiritual authority given to us as co-heirs to God's Kingdom through Christ (Romans 8:17) to bind the plans of evil in a particular situation and then loose God's plans to come against it. When we bind something, we declare it to be unlawful based upon the Word of God. When we loose something, it must be done in accordance with God's Word and in the name of Jesus.

In Matthew 18:18-19, Jesus says:

> *"Truly I tell you, whatever you bind on earth will be bound in heaven, and whatever you loose on earth will be loosed in heaven. Again, truly I tell you that if two of you on earth agree about anything they ask for, it will be done for them by my Father in heaven."*

There was one woman who was so ill her immune system was weakened, and she couldn't be around other people because they might make her even sicker. She constantly wore a medical face mask, and her entire body shook as a result of her ailment. She couldn't attend church, but she was brought in to the office where the leadership of the church prayed for her. They bound the enemy off of her body and loosed God's love and healing power onto her body.

Moments later, she sat up on her own. Then she stood. Her body stopped trembling. That afternoon, she went out to a restaurant with her daughter. The sickness and immune deficiency were gone!

We can also apply this prayer to ourselves. I bind myself to God's love and loose myself from aggravating passions. I can declare that sickness and disease are far from me, loosing their hold because they were bound to me. I can loose the enemy from my life and bind myself to God and His Word. The prayers of binding and loosing are incredibly powerful and, like the prayer of imprecation, exceedingly liberating.

Notes

1   What is Prayer? https://billygraham.org/answer/what-is-prayer/

2   Practical Steps in Learning How to Adore God. http://www.prayerclosetministries.org/assets/PDF/Practical%20Steps%20in%20Learning%20How%20to%20Adore%20God.pdf

2

Knowing What, How, Where, and When to Pray

"Let us draw near to God with a sincere heart and with the full assurance that faith brings, having our hearts sprinkled to cleanse us from a guilty conscience and having our bodies washed with pure water. Let us hold unswervingly to the hope we profess, for he who promised is faithful."

Hebrews 10:22-23

"'Our Father in heaven, hallowed be your name, your kingdom come, your will be done, on earth as it is in heaven. Give us today our daily bread. And forgive us our debts, as we also have forgiven our debtors. And lead us not into temptation, but deliver us from the evil one.'"

Matthew 6:9b-13

The most effective way to pray is when we are in a place of discernment and connectivity with God and the truth where our total dependence is upon the Holy Spirit. Any self-serving motive or selfish ambition is gone, replaced by a total reliance on the Lord that comes from a sincere heart, not from our emotions. This is when our faith makes us fully assured that He will hear, listen, and respond because He has promised to be faithful.

PREPARING TO PRAY[1]

Even though they had followed Jesus for three years, Christ's disciples still felt the need for direction in knowing how to pray. It makes sense. They surely saw the impact of Christ's relationship with His Father and wanted that, too. They wanted to emulate their Lord, to connect with heaven the way He did.

In Matthew 6, Jesus responded to their request by pro-claiming the model prayer, commonly referred to as the "Lord's Prayer." It serves as a recipe that demonstrates how to pray and provides the ingredients that should be included in our prayers. In the first part of the prayer, we direct our worship toward God through expression of a pure heart relationship that is succumbed to His will:

- **"Our Father in heaven..."** This is our initial approach to the Lord where we come with an offering of thanksgiving, praise, love, respect, and the trust that He deserves.
- **"...hallowed be your name..."** God is holy, and His Name is holy. He is worthy of our worship.
- **"...your kingdom come..."** The expansion of God's Kingdom is important to Him, and since we are to

His ambassadors on earth, it should also be a priority
to us.

- **"...your will be done, on earth as it is in heaven."** He
  is the ruler of heaven, and our prayers affirm that we
  want Him to rule in this world. In addition, His will is
  to be paramount in our lives.

Next, we have the opportunity to come to the Lord with
our requests:

- **"Give us today our daily bread."** This "bread" is
  bigger than food or clothes. It encompasses any
  sustenance that He would have for us, or anything
  that we want Him to show us. It can also include the
  needs of others—all sought with the expectation
  that His blessings will make up the difference where
  we fell short in the past, where we find ourselves in
  the present, and where we hope to go through His
  promises for the future.
- **"And forgive us our debts..."** "Debts" are sins, and
  sin separates us from a holy God. John 9:31 tells us
  that "God does not listen to sinners. He listens to the
  godly person who does his will." Any unrepented sin
  may block God from hearing us.
- **"as we also have forgiven our debtors."**
  Unforgiveness is a sin. Mark 11:25 teaches, "When
  you stand praying, if you hold anything against
  anyone, forgive them, so that your Father in heaven
  may forgive you your sins." Refusing to forgive others
  will cause our Father in heaven to not forgive us.
- **"And lead us not into temptation, but deliver us
  from the evil one."** We are to declare to the Lord,

"Don't allow me to do evil. Stop me before I do anything that would destroy my relationship with you and undermine the future that you have for me. Whenever I do anything that is against your will, I will repent."

Traditionally included in the Lord's Prayer, but not quoted in Matthew 6, is the benediction, "For yours is the kingdom, and the power, and the glory, forever. Amen." This recognizes God's authority in heaven and on earth as the King of kings and Lord of lords. Our God dominates, and He bestows that domination upon us! By recognizing His Kingdom authority as we pray, we get connected to it.

After teaching how we can take elements of the Lord's Prayer and expound on each one as we pray, one gentleman who had spoken the prayer since he was a little boy started with, "Our Father in heaven" and expanded it. First, He envisioned the Lord in His heavenly realm as we know it from descriptions in the Bible and praised Him. But then he saw beyond that to all of the heavens, including the planets and galaxies, and realized all of it was God's realm, and that the Lord was even bigger than all of that. It broadened his perception of God's vastness and love. After he spent several more minutes focusing his prayers on that phrase, he moved on to the next one in the prayer and enlarged it, thinking of all the facets of God's holiness.

Acceptable prayer must be sincere and offered with reverence.

He ended up spending 75 minutes with God before finishing his amplified Lord's Prayer. He said it was life changing—and it is, anytime we stretch and multiply our perception of our incredible God.

ACCEPTABLE PRAYER (WHAT TO PRAY)

Acceptable prayer must be sincere and offered with reverence, godly fear, and a humble sense of our own insignificance as creatures and unworthiness as sinners, all while knowing that God loves us dearly and without limitation. It is to be spoken in earnest persistence (Matthew 7:7-8) and an unhesitating submission to the divine will of God. Acceptable prayer must also be rendered in faith (Matthew 21:22; Mark 11:24) that God is the hearer and answerer of prayer who will fulfill His Word and given in the name of Jesus (John 14:13-14; John 16:23-24). As Christ declared:

> *"You did not choose me, but I chose you and appointed you so that you might go and bear fruit—fruit that will last— and so that whatever you ask in my name the Father will give you." (John 15:16)*

Too often, people will get themselves into a rut, believing that God wants to hear only prayers that "sound" holy. They get lost in using overly spiritual verbiage, eloquent prose, or even intentionally trying to appear more consecrated than others through their actions or the words they use. This happened during the time of Christ and was condemned by God (Matthew 6:5-7). Yet God seeks honest, genuine prayers poured from a heart dedicated to Him. After all, He already knows the exact condition of your life even before you speak.

James Ford, former chaplain to the United States House

of Representatives, told *Leadership* journal[2] of a time when he decided to sail the Atlantic Ocean but was caught in a hurricane. As the waves grew and the winds pounded, he got scared but was hesitant to pray. "I wanted to pray for God to stop the storm, but I felt guilty 'cause I'd voluntarily gotten into this. Finally, I came up with a marvelous prayer, seven words: 'O God, I have had enough. Amen.' Within half an hour of that simple prayer, the sky in the west lifted, and there was blue sky."

When you have open and sincere dialogue with God, your prayers will be acceptable and gloriously answered. Here are a couple of other points to remember about acceptable prayer:

1. **Thinking is not praying.** There is a difference between thinking about something and actually praying and having a conversation with God. Sometimes we'll think, "Well, Lord, you know what I'm thinking, so I don't need to talk to you about it." But you can't think yourself into a blessing. God requires us to pray. Scripture says, "You do not have because you do not ask God." (James 4:2) Acceptable prayer is directed to God, acknowledges His existence through relationship, and requires trust.[3]

2. **Praying is not wishing.** A wish is a desire or a longing for something, but that's all it is. It doesn't have form or direction. A wish is not rooted in reality. You can wish upon a star—or you can do as the Word directs and take your desire to the feet of the bright Morning Star (Revelation 22:16) where your wish is transformed into a living hope that, if found in alignment with His will, will be fulfilled.

46

CONDITIONS FOR ACCEPTABLE PRAYER

Even though prayer is open and honest communication with God, it does require that certain conditions are met in order to ensure a positive response from Him. Understanding these conditions will help you to receive and achieve the very best in your communication with the Lord.

Sometimes when people pray they either do not hear from God right away or they don't get the answer they expected. This may cause some people to believe God has rejected them. That isn't necessarily true. Although the Lord does listen to our prayers and is influenced by them, we must remember that our prayers are *requests* subject to His sovereign will. A good father always listens to his children, but he does not do everything they ask. Rather, he responds in the way he knows is best. The same is true of God. As Matthew 7:11 says:

> *"If you, then, though you are evil, know how to give good gifts to your children, how much more will your Father in heaven give good gifts to those who ask him!"*

Others view prayer as being a kind of "remote control" of God. Just push the buttons and He'll do whatever we say. However, God is sovereign—meaning that He and only He possesses supreme and ultimate power and control. He has all wisdom and all knowledge. He knows the future. So, while He allows Himself to be influenced by our prayers, He will do what is best for the whole world and for all time. We may be praying for sunshine while a farmer is praying for rain. We must be humble, submissive, and aware of God's ultimate authority.[4]

You'll recall my earlier story from my book *Astronomical Leadership* when I first realized Tucson was a beautiful place. After we moved to the city, there was another time I was feeling dissatisfied being there. As we sometimes can, I had my blinders on and was only seeing what I wanted to see instead of looking at my situation from God's perspective. As I prayed about possibly moving away from Tucson for another professional opportunity, God gave me a vision of, of all things, a fruit pie. I discerned that it belonged to someone else, but that I was trying to eat from that pie. The Lord said, "That is not what I have for you. It is for somebody else." When I came out of the vision, I wept. I knew God wasn't going to give me what I was asking for. He had a different, bigger plan.

Today, having seen that plan unfold, I'm so glad He showed me the pie I could not have so that I didn't depart from the place and purpose He had for me. Many things—including this book—may not have happened had I chosen to go somewhere else. As Isaiah 55:8-9 declares:

> "'For my thoughts are not your thoughts, neither are your ways my ways,' declares the Lord. 'As the heavens are higher than the earth, so are my ways higher than your ways and my thoughts than your thoughts.'"

I've identified six primary conditions for prayer.

1. **Pray in the name of Jesus.** By praying in Jesus' name, we recognize that Christ has already paved the way for us to have direct access to the Father. When we use the name of Jesus, we infuse our lives with His authority, position, and power. Anyone who believes in the death and resurrection

of Christ as full payment for their sins and has received Him as their personal Lord and Savior is granted that right to approach the throne of grace of Almighty God (Hebrews 4:16).

We also pray in Jesus' name because He has justified us by willingly choosing to sacrifice Himself, take on our sins and die in our place, and, in doing so, forever remove the hold Satan and his fallen angels had on our lives (Romans 3:24-26). By becoming our justification, we can now walk free of all of the enemy's condemnation (Romans 8:1). Therefore, having been justified from all sin, we have to ability to freely go before God in prayer with a clear conscience, a clean spirit, and no burden from any sin.

Finally, we pray in Jesus' name because He is our life and our propitiation, or atonement, for sin. That means that Christ made possible reconciliation between God and humankind. Some of us have a hard time letting go of our sins because they seem so great. They wonder, "How can God possibly forgive me?" But because Jesus is our propitiation for sin, that question is rendered moot by the grace of God. The lies of the enemy cannot steal the relationship we now have with Him. Galatians 2:20 declares:

> *"I have been crucified with Christ and I no longer live, but Christ lives in me. The life I now live in the body, I live by faith in the Son of God, who loved me and gave himself for me."*

We no longer have to be concerned about what we did in the past. The curse of our sins was eliminated forever at the cross.

Praying in the name of Jesus will have incredible outcomes. During the summer in Tucson, there can be powerful monsoon storms that cause dangerous flash floods and property damage. One such storm brought rain and hail that left cars half submerged in water and dented by the ice stones. The next afternoon, as the clouds started building up once more and the skies darkened, two women came together. "We've already been through this once," one said, referring to the entire community. "We shouldn't have to do it again. Let's pray and move these clouds back."

Right where they stood, they boldly held hands and closed their eyes. "Lord," the other said, "by faith and in the name of Jesus, we talk to this cloud and say to it, 'You will not form a storm, and you will not come over this place. You can't come and create damage here. It is not allowed, in the name of Jesus.' The ladies went back to work, and within an hour, not only was the storm formation gone, but it had been replaced with clear, blue skies all around.

What storms, literal or emotional, need to be removed from your life right now? Pray in the name of Jesus and watch God work.

2.   **Pray by faith and with sincerity.** Our prayers are activated by faith, which is crucial since without faith, our prayers will not be answered (Hebrews 11:6). When we trust and believe in Jesus, God the Father welcomes us and gives us the opportunity to come into His presence. Sincerity is paramount in Scripture. Not only does the passage heading this chapter affirm this, but the Bible teaches that our love must be sincere (Romans 12:9; 2 Corinthians 6:6; 1 Peter 1:22) and that we must be on guard to not be drawn away from sincere thinking and pure devotion to the Lord (2 Corinthians 11:3). God demands our heartfelt, genuine prayers.

A pastor prayed with sincerity for a woman and her two kids who were about to be kicked out of their home as the result of a judge's ruling against them. Things didn't proceed as quickly as the pastor had hoped, but she still believed God was going to take care of this family. In her concern, she decided she was going to forego paying her own mortgage that month and

> **Praying in the name of Jesus will have incredible outcomes.**

instead cover the other woman's mortgage payment. Just as the pastor was getting ready to send the money, she received a check in the mail from someone else. It was for the exact amount needed for the woman's mortgage. Thrilled at God's timely, miraculous provision in response to her faith-filled, heartfelt prayers, the pastor was able to pay for both mortgages.

3. Pray in righteousness. The prayers of the righteous person, one who justified by Christ and is therefore in "right standing" with God, are both powerful and effective.[5] Proverbs 15:29 promises that God hears the prayers of the righteous person who stands in awe of His majesty, greatness, goodness, and power. James 5:16 additionally exhorts the righteous to confess their sins to one another and pray for each other so that they may be healed.

Dr. Laura Thompson was such a righteous person. It was not uncommon for her to pray and fast for 40 days, using only a wet cloth in her mouth to obtain liquid. One day she was holding a special service, and a lady who had been in a wheelchair for years was brought to her. The woman was so overweight it took several men to get her into the church and up to the platform. After she was done preaching, Dr. Thompson went up to the woman, heard her story of how long she had been in her condition, then prayed the prayer of a righteous person. Dr. Thompson then declared, "Alright. Get up!"

Because of her weight and weakened state, it was a struggle at first. People around her had to help her rise from the wheelchair. She took one step forward. Then another. Next thing we knew, the woman was walking from the front of the church to the back. When she was ready to leave, one of the men offered to help her down the outside steps. "No," she responded. "I'll do it myself." She did—then she went out for a meal with friends. The next day she drove to the grocery store, walked its aisles, and got what she needed. She was healed by God through the prayers of the righteous.

4. Pray with forgiveness. It may be difficult to choose to operate in obedience as God requires us to forgive, but Colossians 3:13 states this condition of prayer so beautifully. It says:

"Bear with each other and forgive one another if any of you has a grievance against someone. Forgive as the Lord forgave you."

Forgiveness often goes against what seems natural to us, but we must forgive whether we feel like it or not. We do so by placing our trust in God to do the work that needs to be done within us so that our forgiveness will be authentic and complete.

I recall a woman who had been mistreated by her father for a long time. He was disrespectful and sometimes verbally abusive, and this wounded daughter carried the burden of that hurt, refusing to forgive him. One morning in church she approached the altar to pray. She was weeping.

God told the pastor, "Ask her about her father." He did, and the woman's eyes got really big.

"How did you know?" she asked.

The pastor simply responded, "You need to forgive him, don't you?"

She began to cry again. "Yes."

"Are you ready to forgive?" the pastor inquired.

"No," the woman said honestly. "I don't want to."

"But you have to because that is where your biggest blessing will come. God will show favor on you, and He will forgive you, too."

They talked for a few more minutes, then the woman got down on her knees, bowed her head, and asked God to help her forgive her father.

She walked out of that service a totally different woman. It turned out her mother was in attendance as well, and when the pastor told her what had happened, she was amazed.

The Lord will do the work if you just trust Him with it.

5.   Pray in alignment with the will of God. This condition requires wisdom from God, believing that He is gracious and willing to give us insight to know His will so that our prayers will be in agreement with His purposes. Praying according to the will of God includes asking for wisdom (to know His will) and asking in faith (to trust His will). James 1:5-6 declares:

> *"If any of you lacks wisdom, you should ask God, who gives generously to all without finding fault, and it will be given to you. But when you ask, you must believe and not doubt, because the one who doubts is like a wave of the sea, blown and tossed by the wind."*

Another daughter was praying for her father who had chronic lung disease. He had smoked cigarettes most of his life and it slowly took away his ability to breathe. Eventually, he was so weak that he couldn't even walk. She kept praying for him to be healed, and many others joined her in faith. Ultimately, though, the daughter came to a point where she admitted, "I want to be in alignment with the will of God for my father. I don't want to fight it anymore." Then she said of her father, "I want him whole." Later that same week, he passed away peacefully.

It's never easy to surrender our will to His, but when we do, He brings blessing, even in the midst of tragedy. God's purposes are always best.

   6. Never give up. We are to persevere in prayer and pray with persistence. We don't quit or become dejected just because the answer has not been received immediately. Whether His answer is "yes," "no," or "wait," a major element of prayer is the ability to accept God's judgment, submit to His timing, and still continue to pray. Be encouraged by this teaching from Christ in Luke 18:1-7:

> *"Jesus told his disciples a parable to show them that they should always pray and not give up. He said: 'In a certain town there was a judge who neither feared God nor cared what people thought. And there was a widow in that town who kept coming to him with the plea, "Grant me justice against my adversary." For some time he refused. But finally he said to himself, "Even though I don't fear God or care what people think, yet because this widow keeps bothering me, I will see that she gets justice, so that she won't eventually come and attack me!" And the Lord said, 'Listen to what the unjust judge says. And will not God*

bring about justice for his chosen ones, who cry out to him day and night? Will he keep putting them off? I tell you, he will see that they get justice, and quickly. However, when the Son of Man comes, will he find faith on the earth?'"

The King James Version rendering of James 5:16 says that the "effectual fervent" prayer of a righteous person "availeth much." While "effectual" refers to something sufficient to produce a desired result, "fervent" means impassioned, vehement, or spirited. When we apply that type of veracity to our prayers, it helps them become persistent and persevering. This involves far more than simply whipping up our emotions or generating exciting sounds or words. Prayers that never give up express an intense confidence in God that falls in line with the words of Jeremiah: "You will seek me and find me when you seek me with all your heart." (Jeremiah 29:13)

ENTERING GOD'S PRESENCE (HOW TO EARNESTLY ENCOUNTER GOD THROUGH PRAYER)

The keys to unlocking the portal through which we enter into God's presence are very specific.

Key #1: We must know God has already made the way and has invited us to come.

Key #2: We must act on what He has told us.

Key #3: We must stand firm, fighting to take possession of that which He has promised.

Key #4: We must seek Him with all of our heart.

Key #5: We must be able to leave the realm of time and enter the realm of eternity.

God exists from the beginning of the foundation of the

world all the way to the end. We exist in time so that we can count our days. We need the mindset that, as we pray, we move beyond time and into the eternal. This requires us, as much as we are able, to abandon all thoughts of time and the burdens it puts on us. Whatever seems critically important will just have to wait when it's time to enter God's presence. We must forget our clocks and our schedules to completely let go of this realm and experience His eternal realm.

> **Prayers that never give up express an intense confidence in God.**

The Lord does not randomly decide to reveal Himself to any particular person. Anyone who hungers for Him and seeks Him will find Him. The more intense the hunger to seek, the stronger His presence will be manifested. The quantity and quality of our seeking will determine the degree of His revelation to us. You actually hold the throttle in your hands. The question that you have to ask and answer is how much of God do you really want.

As Jesus declared in His Beatitudes:

"Blessed are those who hunger and thirst for righteousness, for they will be filled." (Matthew 5:6)

And later, in His Sermon on the Mount:

"Seek first his kingdom and his righteousness, and all these things will be given to you as well." (Matthew 6:33)

Your prayer time is an encounter with God. Your petitions to Him are a by-product of that encounter.[6] Best of all, God has already positioned you to have that encounter whenever you approach Him. Ephesians 2:4-6 tells us:

> *"Because of his great love for us, God, who is rich in mercy, made us alive with Christ even when we were dead in transgressions—it is by grace you have been saved. And God raised us up with Christ and seated us with him in the heavenly realms in Christ Jesus."*

This is how we are able to move beyond time and into the eternal. This position in heaven belongs to us right now. It doesn't come after we die. Therefore, it is not necessary to beg God or even ask Him for access to the heavenly realm because He has already given it to us. We simply need to believe it, then stand firm in our faith to take possession of what God has made available. Otherwise, Satan will attempt to steal it from us—not by actually taking away our access (he can't do that), but by making us think we've somehow lost it or are not worthy of it.

We must act on what we believe, confident that His Word is sure. We are not orphans. We are God's children. He made a promise to be with us always. He also promised that He is in us and we are in Him. That means it is up to us to take possession of His promise.

All life and blessings come from the presence of God. It is the root source of every good thing. It is where eternal riches that never pass away are found. The devil knows that anyone who finds this place cannot be stopped from entering into all that God has for them. He also knows that the blessings that come from these encounters with the Almighty will overflow to other people. Therefore, we must determinedly set our faces like flint (Isaiah 50:7) and proclaim, "I will take all of what God has given to me. I will possess His presence and I will not turn back until I have what I have requested in my hand." That is the kind of faith that gets results.

Remember, too, that when we pray and enter His presence, God is not coming to our realm. We are entering His. That's what the verse from Hebrews 10 that heads this chapter declares. It is a "new and living way" to God, and it is opened to us by the blood of Jesus Christ (Hebrews 10:19-20). When we enter God's realm, He draws near to us, not the other way around. In fact, He had already made the first move in our direction through Christ's sacrifice on the cross.

As James 4:8 so beautifully exhorts:

"Come near to God and he will come near to you."

The prerequisite for entering into God's presence is simple. We must leave our realm behind. We cannot have one foot in our realm and the other foot in His. This is a spiritual departure, one that takes place when we seek Him with all of our heart (Jeremiah 29:13). Adopt an attitude that says, "I will enter into what God has for me. I will take it by force. Angels are coming through the mid-heavens, pushing aside powers and principalities of the air, coming to take me into the high places, into the realm of God and to the Most High God, into His very presence. That is where I will be and that is where I will stay."

This type of earnest, resolute prayer will result in breakthroughs. What seemed like a struggle before will soon be far removed from you and forgotten. Fear will leave. Anxiety will leave. Peace will come. Joy will come. You will *feel* God's mighty, soothing presence. It is so amazing and awesome that words fail to adequately describe it—and all you can say is, "Thank you, Father God, for coming. Thank you for helping me. Thank you for hearing me. Thank you for your presence."

THRESHING FLOOR WORSHIP AND PRAYER (WHERE TO PRAY)

In Matthew 6:6, Jesus instructed His disciples:

"But when you pray, go into your room, close the door and pray to your Father, who is unseen. Then your Father, who sees what is done in secret, will reward you."

Prayer can happen at any time and at any place, but Christ taught and practiced the example of finding a special place to pray where we can be free of distraction and by ourselves with God. Jesus usually rose early in the morning, while it was still dark, and departed to a "solitary" place to pray (Mark 1:35). Sometimes these places were referred to as "lonely." (Luke 5:16) There were even occasions where Christ went to a mountainside to spend all night praying to His Father (Luke 6:12).

The example is clear. We are to have a special place to pray and connect with God.[7] If you don't have such a place, create one. When I want to steal away from the noise of my life and spend quality time with the Lord, I go to a room in my home. It's about the size of a closet, but big enough for a small lounge seat with "love" and "faith" pillows, and a mirrored table with tissues, pens and paper, different anointing oils, and a little tree with leaves that sparkle. It reminds me of the Tree of Life in Scripture. Everything in my prayer closet is bright, platinum white or gold, and gleaming, including a modest but shiny set of beads surrounding the overhead light that has a dimmer switch. It's a lovely, quiet room where I can sit or kneel. Everything in it has a story and represents the purity, effervescence, and awesomeness of God.

I use it for no other purpose than prayer. It is set aside solely for me and the Lord. It is a place where I go and commune with God. It is my place where I have an expectation to hear Him. It is a place where He will lift me to a place He wants me to be—to teach me, console me, encourage me, and show me what I need to do.

Once you start to do this routinely, God may require you to go to the "threshing floor" to pray and be cleansed. The threshing floor, mentioned 40 times in the Bible, is symbolic for purification. When you have a threshing floor experience, it may make you feel as though you have been through so much that you cannot go on. You may be at a crossroads with God where you are needing to decide to stay with Him or return to where you used to be. Whatever it may be, this is the time to hold onto God and continue to press in, threshing out whatever needs to go (the chaff) until God separates you (the wheat) and positions you for a new revelation or assignment from Him (Matthew 3:12, Luke 3:17).

It is in this intimate "threshing floor" time with the Lord that you realize that whatever storms life may bring, you are assured of a safe harbor and rest with Him. One woman in my church went on a 40-day fast, drinking nothing but water and broth, simply because she wanted more of God and less of the negativity that she felt she was receiving from some specific people in her life at her workplace. She needed to thresh out the chaff of pessimism, cynicism, and gloom and embrace the wheat of joy, peace, and right thinking. During her "threshing floor" time, she said God revealed Himself to her in mighty ways, including dreams and visions. She chose God and spent dedicated time in His Word and tons of time in prayer so she could be cleansed from the negative friends and thoughts and anything else that was unlike Him.

THE PRAYING CHURCH (WHEN TO PRAY)

Finding the time to pray may seem difficult, particularly when you are busy. Work, home, and church responsibilities and demands are everyday realities. Yet when you begin a habit of prayer—be it as soon as you wake up in the morning, immediately before going to bed at night, or even before each meal—it can become part of your daily routine.

Always remember, though, that our prayers cannot be ruled by a stopwatch; they must be governed by an earnest desire to connect with God. Acts 13:22 reminds us that David, while being a flawed person who made a lot of mistakes, was a man after God's own heart. Why? He constantly sought to stay in touch with God through prayer. He didn't keep a particular schedule. He prayed in the mornings (Psalm 5:3), evenings (Psalm 4:4 and 8), and when he was upset or sad (Psalm 5:1-2). David prayed whenever his heart needed comfort or his mind needed direction.

It is possible to have a prayer life just like David's. All we have to do is what David did: praise Him for His blessings, question God with honest integrity, and then quietly listen for Him to respond. Evenings are an especially good time to give thanks to God for being present throughout our day. It'll place us in a mindset to sleep peacefully, trusting that the Lord has answered every challenge and met every need, and that He will continue to do so in the days to come.

We are instructed in 1 Thessalonians 5:16-18 to do the following:

"Rejoice always, pray continually, give thanks in all circumstances; for this is God's will for you in Christ Jesus."

Some believe this is an impossible command to fulfill, considering the number of responsibilities and tasks with which we fill our days. But the scripture does not stipulate that we are to pray without ceasing "unless you're having a really busy day." Rather, it is quite possible to pray continually without making significant changes to our schedules or commitments. How? By shifting our thought processes and turning everyday moments into "prayer moments." Think of it as being similar to keeping music playing in the background. We just need to keep the connection open and talk to God as we go throughout our day.[8]

It is possible to have a prayer life just like David's.

Here are some ways you can do this:

- Begin with gratitude (Psalm 100:4). Tell God what you're thankful for, starting with what He has already done for you.
- Get real with God. Talk to Him the same way you talk to a trusted friend. Just let the words pour out casually, simply, and authentically. Be real.
- Incorporate prayer into your everyday tasks. Let them

become acts of worship by turning them into times of prayer. For instance, as you are folding laundry, pray for each family member or just give thanks for the blessing of your home.

- Pray while you are waiting. While stopped at a light or stuck in traffic, you can turn your car into a prayer closet. Transform such "down" times into something meaningful by praying for the people you expect to encounter that day or the tasks you need to accomplish. Give thanks for your day, and as you count your blessings, you'll make those minutes count for eternity.
- Sing a song of praise (James 5:13). As you lift your voice, offer it to God as your prayer, or even make up your own song of adoration to Him.
- When you mess up, admit it. You have the assurance that when you confess your faults to God, He forgives you (1 John 1:9). Therefore, you don't have to dwell in regret or condemnation. The fact that you are forgiven is enough reason to pray and praise Him.
- Give up worrying. You were not created to worry, yet a lot of your life is wasted doing just that. The next time something is weighing heavily on your heart, envision yourself extending it up to God and letting Him hold it for you. Ask Him to tell you your role and ask if there is something that you need to do. Then do as He instructs and start thanking Him for who He is and what He has already done for you.
- Stop talking once in a while. Keep in mind that the best conversations are two-sided, but you will not hear anything if you never stop to listen.

Notes

1   What are the fundamentals of prayer? https://www.getbi-
    bleanswers.org//prayer-fundamentals.html
2   James David Ford, "Pastoring a House Divided," Leadership,
    Fall 1996, 112.
3   Why Pray? http://www.spirithome.com/why-pray.html#think
4   The Lord hears the prayer of the righteous. http://www.old-
    paths.com/Archive/Davison/Roy/Allen/1940/prayer.html
5   The Prayers of a Righteous Person. https://gracethrufaith.
    com/topical-studies/spiritual-life/the-prayers-of-a-righ-
    teous-person/
6   How I Learned to Enter Into God's Presence. https://
    z3news.com/w/testimonies/how-i-learned-to-enter-into-
    gods-presence/
7   Day 24: Where to Pray. https://www.godlife.com/en/new-be-
    lievers-guide/day-24-where-to-pray
8   How to Pray Without Ceasing. Kelly O'Dell Stanley. https://www.
    crosswalk.com/faith/prayer/how-to-pray-without-ceasing.html

3

When Prayers Go "Unanswered"

"If you believe, you will receive whatever you ask for in prayer."

Matthew 21:20

We generally believe that the only responses the Lord can give to our petitions is "yes," "no," or "not at this time." Yet there are times we may not hear any response at all, and it's in those times of waiting when our faith is tested. But God is our Father—and, as a parent, He has ultimate decision-making authority and knows what is best for us, even if we don't understand the delay or agree with the decision.

Just as good parents will not grant all of their children's requests, the Lord does not give us everything we ask for. But there is no such thing as "unanswered" prayer. He does answer, even if it takes longer than we prefer.

Sometimes I believe we can become so bound by or

stuck in sin that we don't want to hear the answer God is giving us. Perhaps God doesn't seem to be answering our prayer because He is trying to protect us. Maybe our prayer isn't answered by God the way we want because it is not His desire for us. Then there are those times when the Lord answers our prayers, but in a way that we fail to recognize. We pray for prosperity or health, but we receive it in a different way than we originally thought we would.

Whatever the case, God makes no mistakes, even if there are times when we may question His wisdom. God is always "on" and responding in His way and timing. We are the ones who are "off."

Then there are those times when we simply don't know why God has answered the way He has. I recall one woman who had a child with low-functioning autism. He could never be left alone, and sometimes when she turned away from him, he ran away. She desperately prayed for his healing, but it never happened. Now he is an adult, and someone still has to be with him when the woman is away at work. He can never be alone, and she never has a break from caring for him.

This tireless, faithful mom continues to pray—and she recognizes that there's no way she could do what she is doing without God's help. She trusts in His sovereignty and believes her son is a beacon of His light just as he is.

TEN REASONS FOR UNANSWERED PRAYER

If you believe that your prayers are going unanswered, the Bible provides reasons why it may be happening.[1]

1.   **Lack of fellowship with God and His Word.** Jesus promised that if we would remain in His fellowship and

allow His Word to remain in us, we will see results in prayer (John 15:7).

2. Not seeking to please the Lord. In 1 John 3:22 we are told that we receive what we ask for from God "because we do his commands and do what pleases him." This is not to suggest that we "earn" answered prayers any more than we can earn our salvation. He answers our prayers out of His mercy and grace (Hebrews 4:16), not merely from our good deeds. However, keeping His commandments and pleasing the Lord is a product of our obedience to His Word, which is faith in action (James 2:20).

What are His commandments? Mark 12:30-31 tells us where to start:

> *"'Love the Lord your God with all your heart and with all your soul and with all your mind and with all your strength.' The second is this: 'Love your neighbor as yourself.' There is no commandment greater than these."*

John 15:12 adds:

> *"My command is this: Love each other as I have loved you."*

The lack of love and the presence of bitterness and unforgiveness are at the root of many unanswered prayers.

3. Unconfessed sin. In Psalm 66:18, David wrote, "If I had cherished sin in my heart, the Lord would not have listened." Unconfessed personal sin will disrupt the flow of God's blessings and answers to our prayers. There are two main types of sin. Sins of commission are overt, intentional acts of rebellion done in disobedience, while sins of omission are those things we don't do but know we should

(James 4:17). The remedy for all sin is to confess it to God, forsake it, and ask Him to forgive you.

4. **Improper motives.** James 4:3 states:

"When you ask, you do not receive, because you ask with wrong motives, that you may spend what you get on your pleasures."[2]

The motives behind our prayer requests are a concern to the Lord. If our prayers are self-centered or concerned with the gratification of our own desires, then God cannot, and will not, give us what we want. He is not obligated to answer prayers that will merely feed our self-centered, carnal appetites. Wrong motives and licentious desires can be corrected as we draw near to God and purify our hearts in humility before Him. James 4:9-10 adds:

> ## The motives behind our prayer requests are a concern to the Lord.

"Grieve, mourn and wail. Change your laughter to mourning and your joy to gloom. Humble yourselves before the Lord, and he will lift you up."

5. **Not asking in God's will.** God will answer prayers that are in agreement with His will. We can have assurance that those requests will be granted. God's will is revealed to us through the Bible. Any promises found in His Word are a declaration of His will.

6. **Lack of faith.** Hebrews 11:6 declares:

"Without faith it is impossible to please God, because anyone who comes to him must believe that he exists and that he rewards those who earnestly seek him."

Prayer is not merely begging from God. Rather, it is believing Him and His Word! Faith will come forth and grow as we devote our attention to the Word of God (Romans 10:17) and build up our faith by praying in the Holy Spirit (Jude 1:20).

7. Misunderstanding of faith. Remember, faith is believing in the reality of things even though we cannot see them (Hebrews 11:1). In Mark 11:24, Jesus said:

"Whatever you ask for in prayer, believe that you have received it, and it will be yours."

The word "received" comes from the Greek word *lambano* which means "to receive now" (present tense). "Have" comes from *esomai* meaning "to possess later" (future tense). Isn't that powerful? When we pray, we must believe in the finished results of our prayer, and then we will experience the tangible results.

8. Wavering faith. James 1:6-7 delivers the definitive teaching on prayer and doubt:

"But when you ask, you must believe and not doubt, because the one who doubts is like a wave of the sea, blown and tossed by the wind. That person should not expect to receive anything from the Lord."

Those who allow every wind of feelings or circumstances to influence or discourage their faith will not have their prayers answered. They base their faith on situations or emotions instead of on God's Word. Our faith must become stable, steadfast, and consistent in order for us to receive from God.

9. Failure to apply spiritual authority. Some prayers will not be answered until we incorporate the spoken authority of the name of Jesus. Some of the problems we face are the product of an evil, even demonic origin. In such cases, our prayers may need to engage in spiritual warfare to obtain results. This involves calling upon the Lord by name and commanding the spirit to leave, as Paul did in Acts 16:18. There may be other times when we need to authoritatively speak to mountains (symbolic of obstacles and problems) and tell them to move in order to experience the answer we seek.

10. Lack of perseverance. Galatians 6:9 gives us a glorious promise. It encourages:

"Let us not become weary in doing good, for at the proper time we will reap a harvest if we do not give up."

Probably the greatest reason some prayers go unanswered is because many give up praying and believing before they receive their answer. As long as we have the promise of God's Word, be patient and persistent. Keep believing, and don't quit, no matter how long it takes! The Lord will bring the answer to pass.

Two stories of perceived unanswered prayer from Scripture involve David and Daniel. In the first one, David prayed for his baby son to live even though Nathan had told him the child would not survive:

"David pleaded with God for the child. He fasted and spent the nights lying in sackcloth on the ground. The elders of his household stood beside him to get him up from the ground, but he refused, and he would not eat any food with them. On the seventh day the child died. David's attendants were afraid to tell him that the child was dead, for

they thought, 'While the child was still living, he wouldn't listen to us when we spoke to him. How can we now tell him the child is dead? He may do something desperate.' David noticed that his attendants were whispering among themselves, and he realized the child was dead. 'Is the child dead?' he asked. 'Yes,' they replied, 'he is dead.'

Then David got up from the ground. After he had washed, put on lotions and changed his clothes, he went into the house of the Lord and worshiped. Then he went to his own house, and at his request they served him food, and he ate. His attendants

> **It has been said that a prayerless Christian is a powerless Christian.**

asked him, 'Why are you acting this way? While the child was alive, you fasted and wept, but now that the child is dead, you get up and eat!' He answered, 'While the child was still alive, I fasted and wept. I thought, "Who knows? The Lord may be gracious to me and let the child live." But now that he is dead, why should I go on fasting? Can I bring him back again? I will go to him, but he will not return to me.'" (2 Samuel 12:16-23)

Was his prayer for healing "unanswered?" No—God's reply was "no," and when it came, David accepted it and even worshiped the Lord. Can you imagine the faith it took for him to do that at the moment of his loss?

In the second account, Daniel received a revelation about a great war. It came to him in a vision, and it was so terrifying it caused Daniel to pray and mourn for three weeks, during which time he heard nothing from God:

"On the twenty-fourth day of the first month, as I was standing on the bank of the great river, the Tigris, I looked up and there before me was a man dressed in linen, with a belt of fine gold from Uphaz around his waist. His body was like topaz, his face like lightning, his eyes like flaming torches, his arms and legs like the gleam of burnished bronze, and his voice like the sound of a multitude. I, Daniel, was the only one who saw the vision; those who were with me did not see it, but such terror overwhelmed them that they fled and hid themselves. So I was left alone, gazing at this great vision; I had no strength left, my face turned deathly pale and I was helpless.

Then I heard him speaking, and as I listened to him, I fell into a deep sleep, my face to the ground. A hand touched me and set me trembling on my hands and knees. He said, 'Daniel, you who are highly esteemed, consider carefully the words I am about to speak to you, and stand up, for I have now been sent to you.' And when he said this to me, I stood up trembling. Then he continued, 'Do not be afraid, Daniel. Since the first day that you set your mind to gain understanding and to humble yourself before your God, your words were heard, and I have come in response to them. But the prince of the Persian kingdom resisted me twenty-one days. Then Michael, one of the chief princes, came to help me, because I was detained there with the king of Persia. Now I have come to explain to you what will happen to your people in the future, for the vision concerns a time yet to come.'" (Daniel 10:4-14)

There may be reasons we don't know that are causing a delay in the answer to our prayer. Such was the case with

Daniel—but when the answer came, he strengthened himself and moved forward.

ENGAGING HEAVEN

Discouragement about unanswered prayer may cause some to shy away from praying, but prayer is the channel for tapping into the power of God. Prayer gets us on the same frequency with Him and grants us a direct, personal audience with the Lord.

It has been said that a prayerless Christian is a powerless Christian. That's because it is through prayer that we are empowered to enforce the will of God in our lives as we provoke the intervention of heaven on our behalf. The more we pray, the more we are exposed to the manifestation of the Lord's power.

Here are six ways you can ask the Holy Spirit to guide you to pray effectively for whatever need you are bringing to the Lord.

1.   **Pray faithfully**. Hold fast to your relationship with Christ, and pray humbly before God in reverence for who He is.

2.   **Pray decisively**. Don't be wishy-washy when you pray, meaning one day you trust God and the next day you don't. Make a deliberate and conscious decision to agree with the Word of God, and then set your heart to believe it and your mouth to speak it.

3.   **Pray forcefully**. You are not persuading God to answer your prayer. You are coming to take what is legally yours according to the Word of God. Come boldly as a child would to a father.

4. Pray truthfully. There may be times when you are in denial about a situation or have mistaken the facts. Remember to pray in the truth of Christ and of the Scriptures and you shall have freedom (John 8:32).

5. Pray earnestly. Turn your emotions and passions into earnest prayer instead of a hindrance to pray. James 5:17-18 says:

> *"Elijah was a human being, even as we are. He prayed earnestly that it would not rain, and it did not rain on the land for three and a half years. Again he prayed, and the heavens gave rain, and the earth produced its crops."*

6. Pray powerfully. In Ephesians 3:16, Paul prays for you, saying:

> *"I pray that out of his glorious riches he may strengthen you with power through his Spirit in your inner being."*

This power is measured by the standard of God's own glorious riches. His Spirit in us strengthens us to do the things we could never do in our own power, as revealed in the fruits of the Spirit: love, joy, peace, forbearance, kindness, goodness, faithfulness, gentleness, and self-control (Galatians 5:22-23).

To love others as your love yourself, to find joy in pain, to have peace in turbulence, and to be patient and loyal in adversity, you need the power of God. You access that power through prayer, and you revel in that power as you wait for and receive His response to your prayers.

His power also enables you to enter into greater spiritual depths in prayer—which is how we will culminate your journey into phenomenal prayer.

Notes

1   Why Some Prayers Go Unanswered. http://www.victorious.
    org/pub/prayer-unanswered-126
2   Why Doesn't God seem to answer my prayers? https://
    billygraham.org/answer/why-doesnt-god-seem-to-answer-
    my-prayers/

4

Spiritual Depth Through Prayer

"For our struggle is not against flesh and blood, but against the rulers, against the authorities, against the powers of this dark world and against the spiritual forces of evil in the heavenly realms."

Ephesians 6:12

Earlier, we looked at intercession as one of the five expressions of prayer in which we pray for something or someone with purposeful urgency. The person who prays as an intercessor is a great gift to the body of Christ—but they must also recognize that as they intercede, they are also engaging in spiritual warfare.

This battle is very real.

Warfare occurs as the result of unresolved enemy conflict. Where there is no enemy, there is no need for war. Therefore, when intercessors pray, they can come against an enemy, Satan, who will sometimes counterattack in a variety of ways:

- Sicknesses and disease
- Financial setbacks
- Mood swings, bad dreams, or tormenting fears
- Problems in marriages and with children
- Oppression and depression
- Great temptation
- Deception
- Problems among other intercessors
- Disunity in the church, church splits, and destruction

I recall one intercessor who was praying for the deliverance of another person as part of a group of intercessors during a church service. As she engaged the enemy, she suddenly froze. Her eyes and head could move, but she couldn't move any other muscles. It was as though she was paralyzed from the neck down. Another intercessor had to take her by the arm, pull her away, and bring her out of that state. It was a temporary physical oppression manifested as she went into battle. On another occasion, an intercessor was praying and all of a sudden started showing intense anger that was unlike her usual personality. Later, she had nightmares. The enemy responded to her spiritual warfare by bringing mood swings and bad dreams. However, once she and others

When you come against the enemy in intercession, expect that he will attack.

recognized what was happening as the work of the enemy, they pled the blood of Jesus over her mind, and Satan fled.

When we engage Satan and he counterattacks, it takes an intentional, proactive response to oppose him. It is not a time to be passive. When you come against the enemy in intercession, expect that he will attack—and be ready to counter his attack in God's power and authority. Remember the words of Isaiah 54:17 that promises:

> *"'No weapon forged against you will prevail, and you will refute every tongue that accuses you. This is the heritage of the servants of the Lord, and this is their vindication from me,' declares the Lord."*

When we enter into spiritual warfare through intercession, we should be covered by the blood of Christ and be in alignment and agreement with the Word of God. We must be vigilant from the get-go because the counterattack could happen anytime and in many different ways.

THE KINGDOM OF SATAN

It is important to know exactly who Satan is and how his fallen angels, demons, work for him. Although few people personally have an encounter with Satan himself, we have to realize that he works through his army of demonic forces. Just as God is the King of all kings, Satan is the prince over the kingdom of darkness, and he has different levels of delegated authority that work for him.

Ephesians 6:12 reveals those four distinct levels:

1. Rulers. These principalities are a high order of rule in Satan's kingdom and are assigned over geographical regions and nations. Rulers can be described as the master architects over these areas.

2. **Authorities**. These powers have delegated authority under the rulers. They can be described as the contractors who build the architect's master plan (Ephesians 2:2).

3. **Powers of this dark world**. These powers are assigned to conceal the true knowledge of God and of salvation through Jesus. They are masters of human deception, which includes concepts of destitution, lack of light, obscurity, concealment, covering, secrecy, murkiness, shadiness, dimness, and death. These are the powerful influences in the areas of false religions, political mindsets, humanistic philosophies, and man-made traditions.

4. **Spiritual forces of evil in the heavenly realm**. These are the hosts of Satan and can be translated to mean "armies." Their job is to twist the truth of God into a lie. They work to distort man's thinking, character, and behavior against the moral standards of the Lord. They are the frontline demons that oppose the believer's pursuit of God, and they come to oppress and demonize the bodies, minds, and souls of men.

Because of man's fall and Satan's hold in our lives, his demonic works needed to be destroyed in order to take back what mankind had lost in the Garden of Eden. Remember how Adam and Eve talked with God in the coolness of the day, in perfect fellowship with Him. God placed in that garden the tree of the knowledge of good and evil, and instructed Adam and Eve to not touch it. If they did, they would die. Satan attacked, taking the form of a serpent, and put doubt in Eve's heart. She ate from the tree, then gave the fruit to Adam, and he ate. Immediately, their eyes were opened to good and evil. They experienced sin—and at that moment gave away their birthright to rule the earth God gave them. They disobeyed and forfeited their relationship with God, and Satan took that birthright.

But God did something remarkable. Jesus Christ, the Son of God, came to earth in the form of an obedient servant who willingly laid down His heavenly divine authority to operate as a human with earthly delegated authority. His purpose was to exercise great authority and power over Satan. Christ took back the birthright to rule—and restored it back to us!

Since Jesus demonstrated His authority through His total submission to the Word of God, Satan could not touch Him, much less defeat Him. This is played out dramatically in the story of the temptation of Christ. Jesus had entered into the wilderness to fast and pray for 40 days and nights. He was not interceding during this time, but Jesus was engaging the enemy in spiritual warfare. Look at how He responded to Satan's direct counterattack:

"After fasting forty days and forty nights, he was hungry. The tempter came to him and said, 'If you are the Son of God, tell these stones to become bread.' Jesus answered, 'It is written: "Man shall not live on bread alone, but on every word that comes from the mouth of God."' Then the devil took him to the holy city and had him stand on the highest point of the temple. 'If you are the Son of God,' he said, 'throw yourself down. For it is written: "He will command his angels concerning you, and they will lift you up in their hands, so that you will not strike your foot against a stone."' Jesus answered him, 'It is also written: "Do not put

the Lord your God to the test." Again, the devil took him to a very high mountain and showed him all the kingdoms of the world and their splendor. 'All this I will give you,' he said, 'if you will bow down and worship me.' Jesus said to him, 'Away from me, Satan! For it is written: "Worship the Lord your God, and serve him only."' Then the devil left him, and angels came and attended him." (Matthew 4:2-11)

It is in the demonstration of Christ's submission to the authority of the Father through the declaration of His Word that we find it possible to enter into a place under God's authority where the enemy cannot touch us. Our humble obedience to the lordship of God is what diminishes the kingdom of darkness and increases the Kingdom of God.

THE ROLE OF INTERCESSORS

God wants to save people from destruction. In the Old Testament, you'll recall that God sought to find someone to stand "in the gap" (Ezekiel 22:30). Because of the separation and deception sin brought to mankind, the Lord initiated His plan for intercession, or mediation, by instituting high priests as the most important intercessors between humans and God.

In the New Testament, Jesus is our high priest (Hebrews 4:14) and we, as His followers, have become a holy priesthood (1 Peter 2:9) fully positioned and qualified by Him to mediate for others. Therefore, by virtue of the priesthood of Christ, we are all intercessors.

God is not looking for those who can see someone else's sin and faults and then proceed to expose and curse it. Nor is it the job of intercessors to pray that judgment and destruction come upon sinners and rebels. Instead, God is looking for those who can see His plan and then stand "in the gap" as intercessors of His grace—to plead for His mercy until repentance and restoration comes. Intercessors pray and believe that when people are willing to turn to God, His mercy will always triumph over judgment (James 2:13).

CASUALTIES OF WAR

Just as there can be casualties from any warfare that occurs in the physical realm, there can also be casualties of war in the spiritual realm. A casualty of war is any person who is killed or injured in a war by wounds or disease.

War casualties are classified into two categories: hostile and non-hostile. A hostile casualty is any person who is killed in action or wounded by any civilian, paramilitary, terrorist, or military force. Included in this classification are persons killed or wounded accidentally either by friendly fire or by fratricide, which occurs when troops are mistakenly thought to be an enemy force.

> **God is looking for those who can see His plan and then stand "in the gap" as intercessors of His grace.**

Meanwhile, non-hostile casualties are not attributable to enemy action. These occur due to an injury or death from environmental elements, disease, self-inflicted wounds, or combat fatigue.

Here are several issues we can bring upon ourselves to open us up to attack from the enemy as we intercede that cause us to be casualties of spiritual warfare.[1] In every one of these instances, we give up an inheritance that we were given from God (such as being afraid when God has not given us a spirit of fear), and in doing so provide a legal opening for Satan to come in and attack us in that area.

Issue of fear. We do not have to fear the power of Satan as long as we operate within the boundaries of the authority and power given to us by God. In 2 Timothy 1:7, Paul wrote:

"For the Spirit God gave us does not make us timid, but gives us power, love and self-discipline."

Satan uses fear as a weapon against us. We conquer fear with faith in Christ's victory over the devil. Isaiah 54:17 declares:

"No weapon forged against you will prevail, and you will refute every tongue that accuses you."

Issue of authority. The issue of authority is at the core of Satan's rebellion, and the ministry of intercession demands that all issues of authority be settled in our hearts. Mature intercessors understand that God alone has all divine authority. As believers in Christ, we have been given authority to carry out His Kingdom's business by the authorization of Jesus' name. As ambassadors of Christ, we are commissioned to represent Him and have dominion given to us by God (Genesis 1:28).

Issue of pride. Pride is the sin of thinking of ourselves more highly than we should (Romans 12:3). Because of the high level of spiritual activity and revelation received during intercession, we must be on the alert for spiritual pride in our hearts. Pride always leads into deep deception that is difficult, if not impossible, to recognize. Our defense against pride is to walk in humility before our God and to think of ourselves "with sober judgment, in accordance with the faith God has distributed" to us (also Romans 12:3).

Issue of accountability. Accountability is one of the most important things that intercessors need for our protection from the deceitful plotting of the enemy. Intercessors are prime targets for the devil, and it is possible for intercessors to spend so much time in the spiritual realm that they lose their sense of wisdom in the natural realm. Without proper accountability to a higher authority, intercessors may begin to think that others, rather than themselves, are out of touch. As a result, they may begin to judge others as being unspiritual.

Issue of the flesh. Sadly, we can be great at masking the works of the flesh behind a cloak of spirituality. Guilt and shame can keep them locked up in an emotional and spiritual prison. Humility, confession, and repentance are the intercessor's only way back into God's blessings. Just like it was with Adam in the Garden of Eden, only the voice of God calling our names can penetrate the hiding place and bring us back to fellowship with Him.

Interestingly, issues of the flesh cannot be removed by spiritual warfare and rebuking demons. It is only removed when we do what Jesus requires—crucify it. Getting rid of the flesh will automatically remove the demons that are feeding on it. As Proverbs 28:13 tells us:

> "Whoever conceals their sins does not prosper, but the one who confesses and renounces them finds mercy."

Issue of forgiveness. We cannot intercede sincerely for those we have not forgiven. During intense counterattacks from the enemy, even small offenses left unforgiven can become greatly magnified. If intercessors feel tempted to pray judgment rather than mercy, it is probably because they have become personally wounded in battle. Intercessors must ensure that the plank of judgment in their eyes has been removed before attempting to remove the speck from the eyes of those for whom they are interceding (Luke 6:42). Intercessors are to plead for mercy and salvation, even when the ones for whom they intercede have turned against them. Intercessors are to be motivated by the same love that Jesus demonstrated on the cross when He cried:

> **God is looking for those with a humble attitude who will submit themselves under His mighty hand.**

"Father, forgive them, for they do not know what they are doing." (Luke 23:34)

Issue of competitive jealousy. Intercessors are not in competition with each other, but competitive jealousy enters when individuals take their eyes off Jesus and place them on one another. Such jealousy can become very cruel when slander, gossip, lies, and even flattery are used to deceitfully undermine the position, character, influence, and favor of others. We must strive to overcome this type of jealousy through repentance, reconciliation, and honoring one another in love (Romans 12:10).

Issue of unity in intercession. Intercessors are part of a team. They are not lone rangers. They are a part of God's army (not individual soldiers) raised up to possess territories. Unity and interdependence in the army of God are essential in taking cities, regions, and nations. Yet Satan's goal is to divide in order to destroy us (Matthew 12:25). We must choose to walk in love, unity, and forgiveness. Division cannot be tolerated in the realm of spiritual warfare.

We must relinquish all personal battles to the Lord for the sake of the Kingdom, knowing that righteousness and truth will always prevail in the end. As Ephesians 4:1-3 admonishes us:

"I urge you to live a life worthy of the calling you have received. Be completely humble and gentle; be patient, bearing with one another in love. Make every effort to keep the unity of the Spirit through the bond of peace."

Issue of witchcraft in intercession. Witchcraft is an attempt to control others in any of three ways—intimidation, manipulation, or domination—and will become manifest when we enter into spiritual warfare to push our own agenda instead of His. Unfortunately, these three are sometimes used by leaders within a family of believers to try to get them to do something outside of their own will and certainly against God's purposes. Intimidation and manipulation are voiced by, "If you don't do what I say, then I'm gonna do this." Domination declares, "I'm bigger than you." "I'm better than you." "I'm stronger than you." Reining and corralling a controlling spirit is one of the greatest challenges a leader can face.

When someone intimidates, manipulates, or dominates, they are usually not aware that they are practicing witchcraft. However, God is looking for those with a humble attitude who will submit themselves under His mighty hand to do *His* will rather than their own. Intercessors are not to use prayer to coerce others to do what they think should be done. True intercessors pray in line with the vision of the group. Differing visions create "di-vision," and division opens the door for a controlling spirit to operate.

THE LAW OF COLLATERAL DAMAGE IN SPIRITUAL WARFARE

In military action, collateral damage is defined as unintended damage, injuries, or deaths in a warfare setting, specifically to objects or individuals that are not lawful military targets in the circumstances ruling at the time.

A biblical account that speaks to collateral damage is found in Deuteronomy 20:19-20.

> *"When you lay siege to a city for a long time, fighting against it to capture it, do not destroy its trees by putting an ax to them, because you can eat their fruit. Do not cut them down. Are the trees people, that you should besiege them? However, you may cut down trees that you know are not fruit trees and use them to build siege works until the city at war with you falls."*

This law is practical in that it forbids the cutting down of fruit trees that may provide food in later years. Only the fuel trees are to be used to build siege works.

In both physical and spiritual warfare, collateral damage is not only a violation of the laws of war, it is unacceptable to God. The Bible does not allow for the sacrifice of the innocent to save the lives of those in battle. Therefore, we must be careful when we enter into spiritual warfare through prayer to not cut down fruit-bearing *people*.

An example of this from Scripture comes from the story of Stephen the martyr in Acts 7. When we read of his final act of spiritual warfare as he was being stoned to death, Stephen did something incredible to ensure there would be no collateral damage from his last battle.

"Then he fell on his knees and cried out, 'Lord, do not hold this sin against them.' When he had said this, he fell asleep." (Acts 7:60)

Many who read of this courageous act of mercy think that Stephen is only asking God to forgive the members of the Sanhedrin, but his prayer was directed at all those complicit in his death—including a certain young man named Saul who "approved of their killing him" (Acts 8:1) and much worse. Look at what happened the very same day after Stephen lost his life.

"On that day a great persecution broke out against the church in Jerusalem, and all except the apostles were scattered throughout Judea and Samaria. Godly men buried Stephen and mourned deeply for him. But Saul began to destroy the church. Going from house to house, he dragged off both men and women and put them in prison." (Acts 8:1-3)

Stephen's intercessory prayer of forgiveness extended to Saul, who immediately went to work doing everything he could to "destroy the church." His hatred for believers in Jesus Christ, and for what would later be known as Christianity, was notorious.

Yet Stephen must've known something no one else did when he offered that ultimate prayer of forgiveness—for Saul went on to become Paul, one of the greatest evangelists the world has ever known. Much of the New Testament was written by him. By his own testimony, Saul was implicated in the stoning of Stephen, and thus liable for murder. But Stephen was the victim, and accordingly, had the right to forgive any sin against his murderers. Saul was a future "fruit-bearing tree" in the midst of those responsible for Stephen's death, and Stephen's prayer prevented collateral damage upon Saul that may have prevented him from becoming Paul, one of Christianity's mightiest warriors.

Saul certainly didn't appear to be fruit-bearing the day Stephen died. But he was destined to bear much fruit for the Lord as the Apostle Paul. In fact, when he later faced the same fate as Stephen, Paul not only bore the punishment put upon him, but he survived in miraculous fashion.

"Some Jews came from Antioch and Iconium and won the crowd over. They stoned Paul and dragged him outside the city, thinking he was dead. But after the disciples had gathered around him, he got up and went back into the city." (Acts 14:19-20)

Being stoned could have broken his bones and perhaps even crushed his skull. Yet Paul arose, walked to the city, and the next day continued on his journeys. This could only have involved a supernatural healing while the disciples stood over him and prayed.

As intercessors, we cannot judge who the Lord will choose to use in the advancement of His Kingdom. While we are standing in the gap and praying for others in spiritual warfare, we cannot cause collateral damage by assuming that anyone's present behavior and decisions are an indication of their worthiness to be used by God in the future. The Lord is the only true righteous Judge (2 Timothy 4:8). Therefore, He is the only One capable of knowing which "fruit-bearing trees" are in our midst at any given time.

LEVELS OF SPIRITUAL WARFARE

Since not all encounters with demonic forces will occur on the same plane, there are three levels of spiritual warfare.

1. Ground-level warfare (Luke 10:17-20, Mark 16:15-20). This is most common level and occurs daily in our lives. It is at this level that war is waged through salvation, repentance, and the casting out of demons. The avoidance of casualties on this level is dependent upon our right standing with God and our level of faith and maturity. I've seen this

> **Phenomenal prayer is empowered when we "put on" the armor of God.**

level waged many times. Just one example involved a woman with anxiety. We started praying for her and all of a sudden things started manifesting. Her body started to tremble. Her fingers shook. We touched her and said, "Be calm," and we loosed the enemy's oppression on her life. Her body stopped shaking, and she immediately settled down and was at peace.

2. Occult-level warfare (2 Corinthians 10:3-5). The occult is a belief system outside of the Kingdom of God, and it is at this level that demonic activity occurs through words and curses. Curses release the voice of demons who will speak to our minds and in our hearts. Blessings and the Word of God changes these inner voices. Our hearts and minds are the battlefield on this level, and our words are our chief weapons. Casualties on this level can be avoided when we stay free from bitterness, pride, and rebellion.

3. **Territorial-level warfare** (Mark 5:10). This level of warfare takes place over geographical areas such as neighborhoods, cities, states, regions and nations. It is at this level that the rulers and authorities of Ephesians 6:12 are in operation. The intercessory prayers of binding and loosing that take place at this level must be planned and orchestrated from the throne room of God. Earlier in the book, I described a time when our church interceded for Abilene, Texas—but we weren't fighting then. We were praying for a territorial *blessing*. Had we been fighting, we would've engaged by praying against the rulers, authorities, powers of this dark world, and the spiritual forces of evil impacting that city. But we would've done that only if the Lord provided specific direction to do so.

THE ARMOR OF GOD

The armor God has provided us for our spiritual warfare is designed to bring down strongholds in our lives as well as in the lives of others, and is used in the deliverance of the mind from the deceptive power of the enemy.[2] The way we stay free from Satan's deceit is to fight to keep God's love and truth intact while capturing and casting out these lies.

Phenomenal prayer is empowered when we "put on" the armor of God so that we can stand against the devil's schemes (Ephesians 6:11), using the items He supplies to pull down and destroy the enemy's strongholds.

This armor is listed for us in Ephesians 6:14-17.

"Stand firm then, with the belt of truth buckled around your waist, with the breastplate of righteousness in place, and with your feet fitted with the readiness that comes from the gospel of peace. In addition to all this, take up the shield of faith, with which you can extinguish all the flaming arrows of the evil one. Take the helmet of salvation and the sword of the Spirit, which is the word of God."

This armor is not optional since the battle is real. It is for your protection against attack. Let's take a look at each piece.

Belt of truth. Demonstrated through the written Word of God, this is often considered to be the most important piece of God's armor because girding the waist keeps the rest of the armor secure as you maneuver in battle and allows you freedom of movement in the spiritual realm. Without the belt of truth, you place yourself at risk. You must fill yourself daily with Scripture.

Breastplate of righteousness. This piece of armor protects the heart, the righteous consciousness that gives you confidence to stand against the devil when you are being accused. Once you have allowed God's Word to influence your heart and mind, a transformation takes place. Romans 12:2 declares:

"Do not conform to the pattern of this world, but be transformed by the renewing of your mind. Then you will be able to test and approve what God's will is—his good, pleasing and perfect will."

Shoes of the gospel of peace. Without solid footing, the enemy is sure to bring down even the strongest of soldiers. You must be sure of your standing with God and know, without a shadow of a doubt, that you belong to Him and have peace with Him due to your faith in the gospel of Christ. Your feet also take ground from the enemy, and they represent victory. In ancient biblical times, it was customary for the conqueror to place his foot on the head of the one conquered.

Shield of faith. Shields are used both to push against the enemy and to block the blows and fiery darts of the enemy. Your faith in God and His Word, hidden in your heart, will help you press forward and also extinguish the piercing arrows of fear and doubt aimed at you.

Helmet of salvation. The helmet protects your mind, the center of your thought processes. What you think and believe defines who you are and how you operate. If your mind is not in proper functioning order, you won't be able to fight and win. The helmet of salvation ensures your victory in Christ Jesus.

Sword of the Spirit. The sword is the *only* offensive weapon on this list and is the spoken Word of God. This is the specific revelation of God's Word given to you for to overcome a particular strategy of the devil. Romans 10:17 tells us:

> *"Faith comes from hearing the message, and the message is heard through the word about Christ."*

As you become strong and established in God's Word, the sword of the Spirit is activated. You are then able to stand against Satan as one who is unmovable and unshakable because of the truth you carry and possess. The sword of the

Spirit will help you to take back the territory that belongs to you: your health, your family, your finances, and so on.

SPIRITUAL WARHEADS AND ROCKETS

We have been given powerful weapons to use against the enemy. Here are four that act as our warheads to obliterate the works of Satan.

- **Warhead #1: The Word of God**. This is the very thoughts of Almighty God expressed in words.
- **Warhead #2: The Name of Jesus**. This is the single most powerful expression of the love of God, for Jesus *is* the Word of God and truth.
- **Warhead #3: The Blood of Jesus**. Christ's blood represents the essential truth of man's redemption and deliverance from the power of the enemy. His blood eliminated the power of the devil's accusation against the people of God.
- **Warhead #4: The Cross of Jesus**. The cross is where His blood flowed and where the charges against us were erased. It represents the very reconciliation of God.

Of course, these warheads are strong, but they must be mounted upon rockets to get them to their target. We launch these rockets with our mouths by doing the following:

Prayer. This releases the weapons of God into the spiritual battlefield in heavenly places.

Praise. This is magnifying God with our lips.

Preaching. This is proclaiming the thoughts and Word of God to others.

Testimony. This is our witness to the salvation of God in our lives.

Confession. This is proclaiming the truth of God's Word in the face of opposition and trouble.

Prophesying. This activates the revealed will of God by speaking forth the Word of God through divine unction, releasing the potential of God into a situation.

Blessing. This is speaking forth God's divine destiny and favor in people's lives.

Child of God, you have been entrusted with God's delegated authority as His ambassador in this earth realm. You have been given authority in His name to carry forth this great gospel. You have been given power over the evil one. You don't need to fear any of Satan's weapons nor anything that he has fashioned against you as long as do not allow yourself to be caught up in sin, disobedience, or unbelief.

This battle is not yours. It is the Lord's. As an intercessor, it is vital for you to understand your role and operate within your delegated scope and boundaries while trusting that Christ Jesus is leading you to victory.

In the end, your greatest threat in spiritual warfare is not from the devil, but from your own fleshly weaknesses. Never become a casualty of war. Remain humble and under the mighty hand of God while staying constantly obedient to His will and commands.

Notes

1   Intercession and Spiritual Warfare. E. Keith Hassell. https://sermons.faithlife.com/sermons/20445-intercession-and-spiritual-warfare

2   Read Joyce Meyers' book, "Battlefield of the Mind," for greater insight.

5

Activating Who You Are

"Truly I tell you, unless you change and become like little children, you will never enter the kingdom of heaven."

Matthew 18:3

The definition of the word "activate" speaks about creating and converting a substance into action or formally instituting something. It is the state of releasing a possibility—of looking at moving something from one position to another in a quick movement, making it go faster than it was, or of producing and evolving.

In short, to activate something is to make a change.

Activating is not a reactive response. It is proactive. So, if you look at activating who you are through a lifestyle of phenomenal prayer, that means choosing to change by connecting with God in prayer, which in turn connects you to an infinite, eternal realm for your future. It connects you to a power source and a place that you haven't yet seen. It results in action from heaven on your behalf.

Most of all, the power that you choose to activate *is already within you*. The power of God, the will of God, and everything that God has for you is already there. Simple, unblemished faith, like that of a child, is the change required so that you can access the Kingdom currency you already possess in abundance and pay for things in the eternal realm.

Phenomenal prayer, as declared in this book, is how you activate who you are.

Be transformed, and you'll never be the same.

59307498R00060

Made in the USA
Middletown, DE
15 August 2019